D0554078

SKIING DOWN EVEREST

SKIING DOWN EVEREST

Ingrid Cranfield

First published in 1983 by Severn House Publishers Limited,
4 Brook Street, London W1Y 1AA

© Ingrid Cranfield 1983

British Library Cataloguing in Publication Data

Skiing Down Everest and other crazy adventures
1. English art and humour   2. Adventure and
adventurers — Anecdotes, facetiae, satire, etc
I. Title
827'914'080355   PN6231.E3/

ISBN 0 7278 2032 X

All rights reserved. No part of this publication may be
reproduced, stored in a retrieval system, or transmitted in
any form or by any means, electronic, mechanical, photo-
copying, recording or otherwise without the prior
permission of Severn House Publishers.

Typeset by TJB Photosetting, South Witham, Lincolnshire

Printed in Great Britain by Anchor Press Ltd, and bound by
Wm. Brendon & Son Ltd, both of Tiptree, Essex.

For D.

Lustig in die Welt hinein
gegen Wind und Wetter!
Will kein Gott auf Erden sein,
sind wir selber Götter!

'The world is wide, the seas are green,
Yet hills and mountains I have not seen,
Here in my chair
I sit and stare,
What shall I do, O brother?'

– Anon.

IRRATIONALE

Even if you were Chris Bonington or Chay Blyth, you might find it difficult to persuade the public that your adventures have some value. Of course, they'd seem worthwhile to you: posing new technical difficulties or opening up untried routes or localities; they'd also allow you to express yourself physically. Returning, you'd feel richer and stronger – and it would be likely that those armchair spectators following your progress would gain vicariously from your activities.

If, however, you were Giorgio Amoretti, who tried to cross the Atlantic on a Volkswagen, or Rory McCarthy, who goes hang-gliding at vast altitudes from a balloon, you'd probably have trouble convincing yourself of the worth of your endeavours. What would you gain (apart from the rewards of curiosity satisfied and a transient newsworthiness) from driving a motorcycle up Aconcagua or 'flying' a hang-glider underwater?

Many of the stories in this book are about adventures that were preposterous in concept and would never have been attempted by anyone in what we like to call his 'right mind'. Others are instances of the heavy hand of fate clobbering what began as a fairly rational undertaking; and some are made extraordinary by their circumstances or location.

Most importantly, all are true – every last one, so help me God. But if, after reading them, you're still not sated with ridiculous notions, you might like to invent your own using the Do-It-Yourself Crazy Adventure page at the back of the book.

CONTENTS

ALL MANNER OF MEANS

Or madly squeeze a right-hand foot
Into a left-hand shoe.
> – Lewis Carroll, *The Walrus and the Carpenter,*
> *Through the Looking Glass.*

HIGHER, FASTER AND MIURA

In 1970, Yuichiro Miura became 'the man who skied down Everest'. He had already been 'the man who skied down Fujiyama and Popocatepetl' and, while doing so, had set up a world record for speed skiing.

To be nigglingly accurate, he skied down part of Everest, starting at the South Col, some 900 metres from the summit, and using a parachute, which might seem a sensible if mundane aid but to him was 'like an airy lotus blossom on the sacred mountain'. Be that as it may, whatever it may, the Japanese adventurer, resplendent in oxygen mask and crash helmet and looking like an equipment manufacturer's display dummy, launched himself headlong down the Lhotse Face of Everest. Two minutes and twenty seconds after his departure, he was 2,000 metres further down the mountain, where he made what appeared to be an emergency crash landing, gouging out several hundredweight of snow from the mountainside as he flopped and bounced to a halt. After that he continued down into the Western Cwm, reaching a reported speed of 150 kph.)

Unlike Everest, Miura was unscarred when he fished himself out of the vast snow jumble. And unlike six Sherpas in the huge team of his supporters who had

9

been killed by a collapsing mass of ice on the ascent, Miura lived to tell the tale, and to append his own somewhat abstract brand of philosophical musing to it. "The end of one thing is the beginning of another" he averred, adding nothing to the sum of human knowledge. "I am a pilgrim again".

GERMANY'S FRUIT AND NUT CASE

Rüdiger Nehberg, 49, owns and manages a confectionery shop in Hamburg. He is married and has a daughter. When a number of people were asked recently what they thought of him, their candied opinions were less than sweet. 'Crazy', 'a crank', 'he's got a screw loose'.

Nehberg's hobbies are adventurous travel, survival techniques and breeding snakes. He is the author of a book called *Die Kunst zu überleben (Survival)** which became an instant bestseller. It is a more than usually comprehensive text, covering the choice of a partner, first (and second) aid, tips for lone women travellers, information on bribery, smuggling and how to procure weapons legally, notes on what to do if you're taken prisoner, interrogated or mugged, how to communicate with indigenous peoples, and much else besides.

Where other survival experts retreat to the mountains and wilderness, Nehberg tries out his techniques at home – in his house, in trees, in the garden. Unusual, certainly, and doubtless his wife complains that he gets under her feet when she's hoovering, but does that make him a nutcase? No. The public opinions quoted above began to be expressed when Nehberg decided to extend his methods to what he thought was their logical conclusion.

*Kabel-Verlag, Hamburg; and also of *Yanonami*, from the same publisher.

West Germany is a highly developed, affluent nation in which survival, if it is ever in doubt, can be quickly assured by a trip to the nearest confectioner's. People survive there not through their own skills but by utter dependence on the goods and facilities of civilisation which, reasoned Nehberg, has in turn so polluted and poisoned the environment as to make it difficult for a man to survive using only his own natural resources. Food, clothing and shelter are bought with money earned by working in commercial enterprises which destroy and disrupt the original means of obtaining those basic necessities. Break the chain and what happens? Suppose one tried to survive without the support systems we take for granted – would it be possible?

In order to find out, Rüdiger Nehberg set himself the task of walking for 1,000 km through West Germany, living entirely off what he could find, without money, tent, sleeping bag, decent clothing, a knife or cooking utensils.

His discipline was to cover 50 km a day. His self-imposed rules were: no begging, no stealing, no poaching. He started in the cool of autumn.

Apart from its singular value, the scheme had some relevance to a subsequent trip he planned to make in which he would spend up to six months walking in the Brazilian rainforest, with no equipment to speak of, in the hope of contacting Indian tribes still untouched by civilisation.

"I had been afraid of what this Brazilian venture involved for a long time," he said, "because I didn't know how I would get by without food. The idea was frightening because I couldn't see any way of carrying several months' provisions with me. On the trip through Germany I discovered that the feeling of hunger totally disappears after two days and the problem of getting food becomes of secondary importance".

The walk through Germany took twenty-three days,

11

and in that time Nehberg lost eleven kg – fifteen per cent of his original body weight. Instead of his usual intake of some 3,500 calories he never had more than about 500. For the first week or so he felt progressively fitter, then, as the journey took its toll – first of fat and then of muscle tissue – his condition began to decline.

"I could of course have made a greater effort to find food. But then I would have had hardly any time left for the walking. I would have taken twice as long to complete the journey and so would have needed even more food. So I lived, as planned, off my own body reserves".

What then could he eat? One source of food was dead animals he found by the wayside – as long as their smell was not too bad. To be exact, he ate one squirrel, four sparrows, two slow-worms, four frogs, a dog, a cat, a rat, a rabbit, a polecat and a hedgehog. For the rest of the meat course, he ate grasshoppers and worms and occasionally water-fleas. Of the plants, hazelnuts and rosehips were best; then there were couch-grass, groats, stinging nettles and mullein roots.

Since he had no knife, Nehberg used a sharp stone to cut carcasses open. A hollowed-out reed from an elder did service as a straw so that he could drink from shallow puddles. He took the pelts from the cat and the rabbit to wrap around his feet. Fresh leaves served as bowls; and, as ladles, tree branches or silver foil from cigarette packs thrown out by passing motorists. Ribwort and camomile juice soothed Nehberg's damaged and aching feet. To reduce body odour, he wore a bunch of peppermint tea leaves on his belt.

Nehberg was attended constantly day and night. A television film crew recorded his progress and the result-ant programme caused a sensation in Germany. The audience rating was twenty-nine per cent – four per cent more than the Chancellor can expect when he makes an election speech! Viewers shuddered to see Nehberg taking shelter during the cold October nights in a hut he'd thrown together in the woods or in a vacant fox-earth. Watching Nehberg swimming rivers and streams (his rules forbade the use of such patently artificial aids as bridges), some were alarmed to learn that fish stocks in all the major German rivers have now dwindled almost to nothing. And many viewers watched, horrified and queasy, as Nehberg massaged the stomach of a ring-snake (which, being a protected species, had to be left alive) to make it regurgitate a dead frog – which he then proceeded to eat. It wasn't until the second-last day of the walk that Nehberg himself began to feel ill. He suffered mild circulatory disturbances, the result of sudden massive weight loss.

Still, when the inhabitants of Oberstdorf, headed by the mayor, greeted him and overwhelmed him with Bavarian hospitality – milk, pretzels, walking boots and a full-blown village festival – he soon forgot his woes. On the following day, Nehbert climbed the Biberkopf (1,100 m) to the south of the town.

CHARIOTS OF SNOW

What is it that makes Spaniards feel compelled to take motorcycles to strange places? (See also *Spanish Bull.*) Psychologists and statisticians might like to ponder the phenomenon; we can only consider the facts of this case.

Five Spanish heads, belonging to Jaume Llansana, Josep Bou, Joan Comellas, Santi Godo and Josep Lladó, were put together and came up with the idea of riding motor-cycles as high as they would go. Aconcagua, at 7,035 metres the highest mountain on the American continent, met most of their criteria.

Crazy? Perhaps, but no crazier, they argued, than the record-seekers whose aim in life is to spit harder, drink more beer or push a car further than anyone else.

The machines they chose were two Bultaco Sherpa T350s, to be ridden by Llansana and Lladó. Ten hired mules were laden with tons of expedition equipment and the climb began. Easier said than done, of course, because much of the gear had to be stored at a kind of 'advance base' at 4,800 metres. Every fifteen kg of material that needed to be transported involved a three-hour upward climb and a half-hour descent for more. Where the mules ended their slog and turned back, that of the motorcyclists began in earnest.

The terrain was frightful: in the lower stages, loose earth and gravel on 45-degree slopes dragged at the bikes' back wheels. Higher up, steep snowfields sucked the machines under. The sight of a mule skeleton in a gorge was an unpleasant reminder of the team members' prospects if they should fall. Once above 5,000 metres, the thinness of the air took its toll: after every five or six steps they had to stop for a breather. Though exhausted by even moderate effort, they found that sleep evaded them. Nobody much regretted having left at the depot the wheel spikes that would have been useful on ice (but not on snow); but when negotiating steep slippery slopes they reproached each other for forgetting to bring a rope. For every leg of upward progress with the motor-cycles, the team made several load-carrying journeys, to and fro. For every step they lurched forward, they slid one back.

Of the two Bultacos, one made it to 5,000 metres; the other to 6,800 metres, where it sank into the snow and refused to move any higher. Three of the group decided for good measure to make a summit bid on foot. At 6,950 metres, only fifty metres from the top, one began to hallucinate. While he began to see fantasy images, the others saw sense, and they turned back. A snowstorm with thunder and lightning enveloped them on the way down to a mountain hut, where they rested. More nights in the hut followed, more frustrated attempts to reach the Bultaco near the summit, more expenditure of fast-draining energy. The motorcycle was hard to locate. It had been buried in the snow for twelve days by this time; only the handlebar was visible, peeping two centimetres above the surface. Four times Godo, his hair matted with ice, tried to start the engine before at last it sprang to life. Bou had a frostbitten foot: a quick descent was imperative.

Just a year previously, six Frenchmen had tried to ride the same kind of motorcycles up Aconcagua, but had attained no more than 4,400 metres. With their Bultaco Sherpas, entirely standard except for the tyres – one had a Pirelli front tyre and a Dunlop at the rear, the other ran on Michelin tyres – Llansana and Lladó had been spurred on to (literally) far greater heights, achieving, for what it was worth, a world record. Current score: Spaniards 1, French 0.

Making Waves
William Neal, of Salcombe, Devon, once crossed the English Channel in an ordinary bathtub. Evidently this proved rather uncomfortable for a man of his sophistication. In May 1983 he was intent on sailing from London to Leningrad in a jacuzzi worth £1,000. His application to get the luxury bath registered as a ship, as the law required, met with some resistance. Neal remarked that the surveyor from Lloyd's Register who had to inspect the 'vessel' tended to 'get a little grumpy about registering baths.'

SEVENTEEN MONTHS ON THE TROT

Now that leisurely sea passages to the other side of the world are becoming scarcer to find and air travel remains expensive, would-be travellers to Australia could try to emulate the unassisted passage brought off by Kevin Bowers. In seventeen months between 1974 and 1975, he ran from Stoke-on-Trent in Staffordshire to Sydney, Australia.

Running to Australia is not something you do on the spur of the moment. Kevin Bowers had borrowed the idea around eight years earlier from his erstwhile coach, the late Percy Cerutty of Melbourne, who had planned to run the distance himself.

The venture was a family, even communal, affair, for Bowers' wife Leona and two-and-a-half-year-old son Zhenka followed him, in a converted Leyland Austin-Morris J4, as far as Istanbul, together with another married couple, who then left to be replaced by another driver and a 23-year-old training companion of Bowers, Barry Bowler, who ran with him for the rest of the distance.

There was plenty of incident: falls, illnesses, snow blizzards, sandstorms, misunderstandings and damage to the vehicle. Stones, or rather rocks, were thrown at the runners with full malice and painful accuracy all the way through Asia. Dogs were a real danger but could normally be frightened off by fierce noises or carefully aimed missiles.

On the other hand, the runners were shown many kindnesses and gestures of respect. "Yugoslavia tasted of plum brandy and pigs' trotters," wrote Bowers, but "in that hot weather the plum brandy was a menace. After 45-50 km in the sun, the last thing I wanted was that so-kindly-meant glass, endlessly topped up. Some mornings I positively staggered about the road as I ran". In New Delhi, word of the runners' arrival having preceded them through the good offices of Road Runners International, they were escorted into the National Stadium by India's leading athletes. By permission of the Lord Mayor of Istanbul, Bowers and Bowler became the first people to run across the Bosporus Bridge, then just a year old. And later, watched by tribesmen armed with rifles, they were the first to run through the Khyber Pass.

The Michelin tyre man on the roof of the van "often aroused curious and respectful attention from villagers... who treated it as our idol". But outside the Red Fort a holy man was "clearly jealous. We found him dressed in paper flowers dancing excitedly round the van and every now and then tapping the feet of the 'idol' ".

And finally there was the sprint across Australia itself, through the ghost towns of Western Australia, the mining towns of Coolgardie and Kalgoorlie, the Nullarbor Plain and the Blue Mountains.

When Kevin Bowers reached Sydney, he had passed through thirteen countries and run 16,462 km.

BOUGHT A CROOKED CAT, SAILED A CROOKED MILE

Francis Brenton was born in Liverpool some time in the late 1920s. During World War II he served with the British Army in India, Burma and Malaysia and with the Australian Army in Korea. Soldiering, hard manual labour and sailing had given him a tough hide, a sound stomach and the ability to live hard. He was slight, wiry and blue-eyed and wore his greying blond hair in a crewcut. He had a thin moustache and a goatee beard. Too busy making friends around the globe to have time for a family, he remained single. In 1953 he settled in Chicago.

In Tenerife in 1961, Brenton paid £239 for a gaff cutter

17

called *Nengo*, 7.3 x 2.1 m, and that year sailed her from the Canaries to St. Lucia in fifty-three days. His total outlay, covering everything he needed for the voyage, was £26. He had devised a system of navigation which, to his knowledge, had never been used by anyone in crossing the Atlantic before. Indeed, he did not know of 'anyone who suspected that this method existed'. Yet numerous mercantile marine and naval navigators agreed with him that the system was both simple and practical. It involved a copy of *Brown's Nautical Almanac*, already on board the boat when he bought her, which contained lists of the times of sunset and sunrise at every important position from 60°S to 60°N, a wristwatch – '*almost* waterproof', and a transistor radio, by which he could synchronise the watch with Greenwich Mean Time. Knowing that the length of the day varied with latitude and that longitude could be measured by calculating the difference between actual time of sunrise and the time of sunrise at Greenwich, he was able – given reliable performance by watch, radio and mental arithmetic – to calculate his position. It only remained to make allowance for the time sailed between sunrise and sunset – easy enough to estimate.

At Jacmel, the Haitian government arrested Brenton as a spy and he barely escaped with his life. His boat and all his belongings were lost. Brenton proceeded on to South America, where he spent some time buying bat droppings (!)

While among the Indians of Santa Marta, in Colombia, he bought a dugout fishing canoe 7.9 m long, hollowed from a log of a cashew tree, and another 5.7 m long built by the San Blas tribesmen of Panama. Back in Colombia, at Cartagena, in 1966, Brenton joined these two hulls with telegraph stay wires to make a catamaran. He filled the interior with stores and equipment, except for a 2.4m stretch from the stern, which he partially covered with a small coach roof and a sliding hatch, under which he could live and sleep. It was a lot less than cosy. When sleeping, he had his heels against one wall of the hull and his knees against the other. On waking he had to stretch one arm and one leg at a time. To the hulls he stepped two 3.7m masts, which cost him $1.43, and attached thereto some homemade sails having a total area of 18.6 sq. m. To his navigation equipment he now added an eight-dollar 'Mickey Mouse' compass purchased in a store in Colombia.

Francis Brenton called his vessel the *Sierra Sagrada*, which loosely translates from the Spanish as 'Holy Mackerel', and in this contraption sailed down the Amazon and out to sea. Hurricane Alma met him on the way across the Gulf of Mexico. This, he wrote, 'nudged me along prettily for days at six or seven knots, when I'd been able to make only three before.' When he arrived in Venice, Louisiana, some 130 km south of New Orleans, Brenton acquired a Johnson 20 h.p. outboard motor, mounted it on a wooden frame between the hulls and with its help motored 2,400 km up the Mississippi, through the Illinois River waterway into Lake Michigan and to Chicago. This took him ninety days.

In Chicago, Brenton came to an arrangement with the Field Museum of Natural History. He was to sail to Africa and there spend six months inland gathering artefacts for the Museum. For some fairly unaccountable reason, he now sold half of his catamaran – one of the dugouts – to the Museum. This naturally left his craft a little unbalanced. To rectify the fault, he built a substitute and put this in the place of the missing dugout. The makeshift outrigger could only be described as a plywood box 6.1 m long and 1.1 m wide, with a V-shaped bottom but otherwise flat-ended and flat-topped. Brenton had intended to make and attach a false bow and stern to this pontoon, but never got round to making the after section. On board he had no heat, nor any means of obtaining hot food or drink, no galley and no illumination system other than a torch.

In June 1967, our self-taught skipper set sail from Chicago through the Great Lakes bound for Dakar, Senegal. On the Canadian part of the trip, which took him down the St. Lawrence River, he ran the motor about twelve hours a day. Putting in at Trepassey, in southeastern Newfoundland, he met a Master Mariner, Capt. G.J. Missing, who listened to Brenton's story, looked at what he called the 'defunct outboard', the 'peeled tree masts' and the whole 'haywire' vessel, and tried to believe his eyes and ears. It was difficult. Yet, stated Missing, "here was Francis and here was a dugout canoe in Trepassey and they did not come by air". Moreover, Brenton was "not a bum or a blowhard – just a bloke dedicated to doing his own thing. His story had to be dug out of him – if you'll forgive the pun". Capt. Missing stocked Brenton's boat up and the *Sierra Sagrada* sailed away again.

Bad weather and headwinds hindered his progress to West Africa. Along the Newfoundland coast he was fogbound and often found himself within fifteen metres of the rocky coast. Five days out from Newfoundland, he lost his precious water tank, which had contained 68 litres of water. Like the French doctor, Alain Bombard, who had sailed the Atlantic and lived off the sea, Brenton had the eccentric idea that a man did not require drinking water when sailing in the high humidity encountered at sea. (Perhaps the body would absorb water through the skin?). Without drinking water, but doubtless enjoying the wine made from sugar-cane flavoured with anise that he had taken on board, he survived for forty-one days before meeting a German freighter, which gave him twenty-two litres of water, food, medical supplies – and his position.

Sixty days later, he drew near a Russian ship, the *Kostroma*, just fifty km off the African coast. Brenton was forcibly 'rescued', being hoisted out of the water before he could protest that all he wanted was an accurate position. The Captain's English was minimal. When Brenton asked him where he was, the good Captain replied: "You on *Kostroma*"! The Russians landed Brenton and his boat at the nearest port. Since leaving Trepassey, he had been 106 days at sea. In December 1967 he hitched a lift aboard a Danish ship and was taken to Dakar, his original destination, where he began his Museum work. On the Atlantic leg of the voyage, the outboard motor had never failed when he needed it and for a time, after the rudder had broken in half, it had been his only method of steering.

All that now remained was to make the trip back across the Atlantic to Chicago! On board the 'raft-craft', as Brenton called his vessel, he carried a pile of silver-coloured fabric. Brenton had theories not only about navigation and drinking water but also about balloons.

The idea was that the balloon, for that was indeed the purpose of the fabric, with Brenton in a gondola slung below it, should tow his boat back to America. Unable to stow hydrogen cylinders aboard *Sierra Sagrada* for the eastwards crossing, he had instead carried 275 kg of calcium hydride.

The cube-shaped balloon, which journalists remarked was 'the only square thing about the venture', was duly inflated and by all accounts shot up rather too quickly, pitching the passenger out of the gondola and straight into hospital. It is not clear why the Spanish Air Force should enter the picture, but it was they who had to shoot the balloon down.

When he had recovered, Brenton rather sensibly abandoned the balloon-tow idea, got back in his boat and in forty-seven days sailed across the Atlantic. Off the Virgin Islands, he was picked up by a Russian trawler and put ashore. There, he noted sadly, he found more empty beer bottles than virgins. After a couple of renewed (disastrous) attempts at relaunching the balloon, he sailed on to the Bahamas, Florida, through the intracoastal waterway and the St. Lawrence and into the Great Lakes. This took another two months and when he arrived back in Chicago, in October 1968, he had again sailed and motored some 24,000 km.

His next job for the Museum was to study how South American Indians treat certain diseases, and to collect herbs and artefacts such as blow guns, in the jungles of eastern Brazil. It did not however entail using his raft-craft, his half-catamaran/half-dugout, his outboard cruiser with its schooner or possibly ketch rig and its tiller or perhaps outboard steering ... Holy mackerel! How *do* you describe it?

Trans-Siberian Russian
Let's not forget Georgyi Bushuyev of the USSR, for whom one heart attack was warning enough. While he was still able, Bushuyev, then pushing fifty, walked across the Soviet Union from the Baltic to the Pacific. The 10,940-km journey, from Riga, Latvia, to Vladivostok, took 238 days in 1973-74.

WHEELERED VEHICLES

In the year 218 B.C. a terrible rumour began to spread amongst the Romans of the Po Valley. Wild mountain people, trembling with fear, told of hundreds of thousands of brown men accompanied by strange beasts 'each one as big as a house' who had suddenly emerged from the mists and snows of the pass in the Graian Alps between France and Italy. Hannibal! With an army said to have numbered originally 100,000 men, the Carthaginian general had marched from Spain over the Pyrenees and

Alps into Italy, raising the Gauls against the Romans as he passed. The great beasts, as modern schoolchildren know, were elephants. Tens of thousands of human deaths occurred along the way. When Hannibal reached the northern foot of the Alps, the arduous march had reduced his force to 50,000 foot soldiers, 9,000 horsemen and 37 fighting elephants. The crossing in October to the southern foot of the Alps, fifteen days of appalling toils, on roads thickly covered with snow and ice, cost the lives of 30,000 more of his foot soldiers and 3,000 of his horsemen. Hannibal, who at the age of nine had been made by his father to swear eternal hatred for the Romans, believed that Rome could be overthrown only in Italy. There he waged the Second Punic War for fifteen years, gaining for a time uninterrupted victories. When, many years later, the tide turned against him and his beloved Carthage, Hannibal took poison and died. The year was 190 B.C.

Now advance to the year 1979, when a 35-year-old philosophy professor from Los Angeles, Jack Wheeler, set out to duplicate Hannibal's feat. Well, not all of it. Even Wheeler – author of a book called *The Adventurer's Guide*, climber (youngest ever to climb the Matterhorn), adventurer (spells of living with cannibals, jungle treks, hunting maneating animals), swimmer (the Hellespont twice) – even Wheeler couldn't rustle up 100,000 men. Instead, he assembled a party that numbered six, together with himself and his fianceé, and, with two tiny circus elephants nicknamed Baby and Chiquita, the expedition ambled away from the French village of Bramans in late September. The alpine paths are as unfit for elephants as ever they were in Hannibal's day, and in places expedition members had to stand along the edge of the trail to distract the animals' attention from the precipitous drops. Wheeler's crossing, via the 2,490-metre Clapier Pass on the French-Italian border, had its anxious moments but in all took only five days against Hannibal's fifteen. Moreover, the Professor lost not a single member of the group, man, woman or beast, and arrived in the Italian town of Susa to a hero's welcome.

BULLDOG DRUMMOND AND THE MYSTERY OF THE PYRAMID

Urban ascent was made criminal trespass in New York City in April 1923, less than five weeks after one Harry F. Young had plunged to the pavement from the eleventh floor of the Martinique Hotel on Broadway. The law has by no means kept pace with the sophistication of those who would break it, but its enforcing arm has grown steadily longer and its eye ever more vigilant. This situation leaves 'builderers' at a loose end – usually several storeys above the ground.

Ed Drummond is a British-born, American-naturalised climber of outstanding audacity, or over-the-top fool-hardiness, depending on one's point of view. Among Drummond's climbs have been a twenty-day ascent of the Trolltind Wall in Norway, during which he and his partner waited in their hammocks for several days until rain replenished their water supply, and a solo ascent of the Nose of El Capitan in Yosemite. In late 1976 he was 32 years old and the owner of a fledgling business called the Bulldog Construction Company which offered scaffoldless steeplejacking for jobs such as goldleafing and sandblasting.

Drummond invited Jeff Long, a climber from Boulder, Colorado, to share in his plan to climb San Francisco's Transamerica Pyramid. This building was designed to circumvent zoning regulations which specified that no new buildings could have a total floor space greater than fourteen times the ground area of the site. At ground level the Pyramid occupies fully half a city block; 257 m higher, it tapers to a needle point. The structure has been called 'too tall for its site, too unconventional for its surroundings and altogether unsuited for a city like San Francisco'.

Drummond had already mentally mapped out the difficulties of the climb: columns at the base, windows up to the forty-eighth floor and a 65-metre spire made of mysteriously lit louvred panels that seemed both solid by day and opaque by night, both grilled and yet smooth.

Naturally, the more closely Long and Drummond studied the problem, the less they seemed to know – and the harder it became to garner information. How far apart were the jutting window frames, for instance? What shape were they? Were there anchors for window cleaners? Would pairs of window frames take a nut, a piton or a cam? How did the windows open? At what height would the climbers be out of reach of fire engine ladders? Supposing the climbers dropped a tool or a rope: on which wall would they be posing least risk to spectators below? Would a Saturday or a Sunday be better from the point of view of spectator safety than a weekday? If the police were to move in, would it be better for the climbers if there were a large crowd or a small one? And what *was* the solution to that last portion of the Pyramid?

Posing in turn as architecture buffs, a team of aspiring window cleaners, lecturers in engineering, and tourists, the climbers tried to tease out what information they could about the building from observation, official records and the authorities.

Needless to say, Ed Drummond had already been refused permission by the Pyramid's managers to climb the building. Secrecy was therefore of the first importance.

One of several reconnaisance expeditions took them to the fifty-second floor of the Bank of America Center two blocks south of the Pyramid. From there they could study their objective with binoculars and telescope. This revealed several new variations to their proposed line of ascent and two or three spots which would conceal them from police observation below; but it provided no key to the louvred spire.

Ed Drummond, by now as high as a kite on his own temerity, was gleaning advice, promises of media coverage and equipment all over town and declaring brazenly that they should not give in to orders to abandon the climb unless the police backed up their insistence by drawing guns. Jeff Long and Drummond's pretty 20-year-old wife, who was to go with them, were less cocksure and persuaded Ed to take a more reasonable line.

Shortly after 3 am on Saturday, 29th January 1978, the climbers began their ascent. Their 'ground crew' consisted of an eight-person film unit, a photojournalist from the *San Francisco Chronicle*, a physics professor from Berkeley standing by as a kind of decoy to button-hole the police with scholarly discourse, and friends with 'programme notes' to be distributed among spectators and authorities and letters to be delivered to the mayor, the police chief and the State governor. A helicopter was scheduled to make two sweeps of the building, filming the performers, at $250 per sweep.

In addition to the cameras, microphones, hammocks, food, climbing hardware and other necessities, the climbers carried a rubber chicken, balloons to be released from the summit and three clown's noses – just to show that they could mix business with pleasure.

The first pitch took them onto the restaurant roof where, slumped against a pillar, they suddenly realised that their only line of ascent passed directly in front of the guard's well-lit coffee room. However, the danger of being spotted soon paled before other unforeseen difficulties. Nylon webbing, intended to help them climb pillars, shredded when it caught on the rough concrete, as did the skin on the climbers' hands. Faced at close quarters with the problem of climbing pillars and glass, Long homed in on a solution, at the same time realising that he was not skilled (or daring) enough to perform the manoeuvre himself. With Ed Drummond there, he need not have hesitated. Drummond lodged himself at the bottom of a pillar with his feet against the smooth glass and 'walked' up the pane, maintaining gentle pressure with feet and rump so that he could nudge his back higher and then rest his feet. Long described the display of steel nerves:

"One misstep, concentrating too much pressure on too small an area of glass, and he would have shot his foot through, leaving one sheared leg on the second floor and his body dangling above the pavement. It was impossible to protect his ascent, so Ed gingerly continued with an even, apelike meditation. I watched horrified as other, equally deadly, consequences to Ed's motions occurred to me, but I didn't communicate this fear to Grace. She lay against the pillar, suffering Ed's boldness without a glance ... Ed's dare was the sleekest, fiercest act I've ever seen, and it worked. With ruthless happiness, he allowed himself to fool the sharp, massive contours of the building, glueing and unglueing his hands and feet and body across the glass ... At last he began to marionette two ropes into position, one on each side of a pillar. I clipped jumars onto these ropes, which by arrangement draped the pillar on either side, and then walked up in opposition to Ed's stance".*

By now they had been on the move for two hours, dawn was sneaking up on them and they hadn't reached the windows. At this point, two janitors inside the building, busy changing lightbulbs, caught sight of them and did no more than wave casually. By standing on Long's shoulders and outstretched palms, Drummond managed to secure stirrups into a seam in the concrete

* Jeff Long: "In the Constellation of Roosters and Lunatics", in *Ascent*.

and forced a way up to the windows. These proved only moderately difficult and were at least uniform. Minutes later Ed was up to the seventh floor, anchored to a window-cleaner's bolt, his stance reinforced with several tube chocks and a specially made wooden piton.

At that moment, a security guard, alerted by someone, sprang into view. Dashing to a vantage point, he scanned the wall, spotted the climbers and went gently berserk with fury. The Berkeley professor stepped forward and tried in vain to soothe him. Repeating the performance with the police later, the professor himself ended up under arrest. The race was now on. Reporters and television cameramen began to cluster below, closely followed by six fire engines and eight police cars. A policeman arrived at Ed's level and set up his radio on a ledge. With pointed politeness, he observed that, thanks to the climbers' irresponsibility, he was unable to respond to calls for help in *real* emergencies. Absurd numbers of police invaded the premises and crowded into the garden, prepared for *something* but too inexperienced in this kind of operation to know what. Grace Drummond finally succumbed to the qualms she had felt all along and Long and her husband lowered her, spiralling, to the ground.

By noon the game was up. A dozen policemen ushered the climbers in through the window at the seventh floor. Two of their number, heartily impressed with their own ingenuity, happily described the plan they had meant to carry out if the climbers had declined to surrender. "Ignorant of the fact that we'd been anchored to the exterior, they blithely described how, with a quick shove on the window behind Ed, they would have neatly tumbled us both into the room". In fact, this would have had the reverse effect. "In horror I imagined the likelihood of officers tumbling to the sidewalk instead".

The officers revealed the human face of policing in their ignorance of climbing techniques; but they went one better than the man in the street in failing to understand how a window works.

And so the uninformed uniformed tightened the noose on the surrendered suspended, and in the battle of twits only the Pyramid came out on top.

Anything You Canoe Do, I Canoe Do Better
The Serpents Tail, Llangollen, Wales, is the venue for the World Cardboard Championships. No, not making cardboard, or throwing it or eating it; canoeing in it. A recent competitor (1981) reported that "the finished boat was of a folded and sewn construction, and looked remarkably like a cardboard box". Having capsized twice at the start, his crew completed the course upside down clinging to the bottom of the boat. Can anyone follow that? Yes. On the Narrabeen Lakes near Sydney, New South Wales, there is an annual Concrete Canoe Race. The vessels are based on the 'ferro-cement' method of construction; to sand and concrete, various admixtures are stirred in – crushed polystyrene with welded mesh/birdwire reinforcement, or glass beads and fly screen mesh. Probably there are places in the world where races are held for canoes made of pure virgin wool or condensed mushroom soup, but these events do not yet have international status and news of them has not reached our ears.

FRENCH DUEL ON THE ATLANTIC

The history of adventure is full of races, mostly of the tacit, unofficial kind. There was the tragic contest between Scott and Amundsen, and the rivalry between the British and, particularly, the Swiss to put a man on top of Everest. Recently, two men – an Australian and an American – jumped into helicopters at about the same time to try to be first to fly such an aircraft around the world (the American won); and at various times during the last two or three years there were no fewer than five teams each with its eye on the first balloon flight around the world.

Christian Marty and Frédéric Giraldi both denied that they were taking part in any sort of race. Instead they stuck to the notion that 'I'm going and he's going at the same time and I'm going to try and get there first'. (To many this might sound indistinguishable from a race). The joint aim of the two Frenchmen was to windsurf alone across the Atlantic. And who won the race? Well, in a sense they both did.

Marty left Dakar in Senegal on 28th November 1981, had mechanical trouble, returned to port and restarted on 12th December. Thirty-seven days, six hours and fifty-three minutes later (18th January), he reached Kourou, not far from Cayenne, in French Guiana. He spent the entire crossing – all but thirty seconds – on his 3.5 metre by 70 cm surf board, and covered 4,200 km.

Giraldi started out from Hierro, one of the Canary Islands, on 9th December, travelled 4,800 km in twenty-seven days and touched land on the French Caribbean island of Guadeloupe on 4th January. Not by choice, Giraldi spent the nights in a berth below the deck of his escort vessel, the thirteen-metre yacht *Soleil et Vent*.

Marty spent two years and a considerable sum of money preparing for the trip. A certain amount of that time was given over to convincing his wife that it could be done – and that he should do it. The money went on first-class equipment. Purists may argue that because he travelled from mainland to mainland and stuck to his surfboard the whole time, his was the first genuine crossing. But Giraldi's was not a bad achievement either – and he did complete his voyage first.

How was it done?

Marty had a supply ship, a motor boat called *Assiduous*, safety dinghies and five outboard motors. There seemed to be a jinx on the motorised part of the expedition, though, for the *Assiduous*'s engine actually fell out during the last week of the crossing, then, one by one, the five outboards failed until not a single engine was working. In the end, there was the risk that Marty would lose sight of his accompanying crew, but he pressed on – and the worst failed to happen. He slept – one or two hours at a stretch – on the board; his escort kept him supplied with food: lots of cheese and dried fruit, together with a rather good French cuisine. Twice during the night and three times while eating breakfast, he was tipped off his board. The escort crew had to start from scratch to make him another meal each time. Only once did he have any problem swimming back to the board and that was when it capsized. The dinghy crew had to come to his aid – and this entailed his stepping into the boat for that notorious thirty seconds.

(When John Ridgway and Chay Blyth rowed the Atlantic in 1966, they spent a few hours on board a passing ship, and wondered whether this lapse would count against them when the ethics of the voyage were weighed in the public balance. Blyth concluded: " . . . the answer is as unmistakable as a palm tree in a pantry. It just will not matter a damn.")

Early in Giraldi's voyage, the outrigger system, which was clasped across the board at night to stabilise it, broke and a little later the clasp fixing the yacht's main boom to its mast snapped. Despite emergency repairs, the yacht could no longer maintain sufficient pace to keep up with Giraldi. Thereafter he retreated to the safety of the yacht at night. There were no dinghies on his voyage. His meals consisted of his normal diet and mineral supplements and he managed to *gain* weight during the crossing.

Both the Frenchmen regard with horror the prospect of crossing the Atlantic again by the same means. (Fortunately no-one wants them to.) Giraldi, who likes chopping as much as he likes changing, has other plans in mind. His previous adventures give little clue to what these may be: he has, for example, roller-skated 900 km from Marseille to Paris in eight days, motorcycled from Marseille to Istanbul, and competed in a 100-km running race. Marty too is looking forward to other things; his windsurfing will be strictly for fun in future. Does it bother him that Giraldi arrived a few days before him? "Not at all" he replies. "Neither of us was the first man to cross the Atlantic – it was Christopher Columbus". In settling one argument, Marty opens up another: historians will be quick to point out the claims of the Vikings, or of a certain Irish monk called St. Brendan . . . (But it's for sure *he* didn't use a surfboard.)

CLIFFERS

It is a well-known fact that mountaineers don't like walking. And by and large they much prefer climbing up a mountain to clambering down. This is tough luck, given that what goes up must come down.

A solution to this problem has been found and put into practice by three Americans. Randy Leavitt, Rob Slater and Will Oxx are said to be the world's only 'cliffers' – truly a rare breed. A cliffer climbs a big wall by ordinary mountaineering techniques, then descends by parachute. Leavitt was the first to achieve this feat by climbing the Excalibur Route on El Capitan and jumping off the Dawn Wall. He landed safely on El Capitan Meadow where he was arrested. He was not released for four days. Oxx, a midshipman at the US

Naval Academy in Annapolis, Maryland, followed suit in the summer of 1981 with a climb of the Salathé Route on El Cap. and a climb-jump the following summer off Half Dome.

Rob Slater soloed the Pacific Ocean Wall on El Cap. in five days, a remarkable achievement since teams able to offer each other mutual support usually spend as long or longer on the route. Slater then parachuted off the top by night! A few weeks later, with Mike O'Donnell and Randy Leavitt, he climbed El Capitan's Sea of Dreams, considered by many to be the most technical and dangerous route in the world. Its so-called 'death pitches' require ten or fifteen belay anchors apiece, all of which would probably be jerked out if the climber fell (thereby negating their purpose). When the climbers had got up eleven pitches, Leavitt broke his fibula and had to rappel down (a descent by a single rope) and walk for 1,200 metres to get help. The others finished the climb later. Rob Slater jumped off the summit shortly before dawn, landing in front of two park rangers, who gave chase. Anyone who performs this kind of jump can expect to fall foul of the law. See *Taking Flight in Yosemite* (p107).Slater jettisoned his parachuting gear, threw himself into a river and got away. At the time of writing, the fate of the parachute gear, which the rangers confiscated, is, like its owner, a bit of a cliffhanger.

JAUME, JOAN, JOSEP – AND JULES

Jules Verne (1828-1905) excelled at combining the fantastic with the real in proportions that differed from one novel to another. Nobody has ever journeyed to the centre of the earth or descended 20,000 leagues beneath the sea, if indeed these two destinations are not one and the same; but in 1980 three Spanish adventurers, aiming to 'stop reading and start living', translated into fact Verne's novel *Five Weeks in a Balloon*. It took them nearly a year.

The Spaniards – Joan Comellas, Josep M. Lladó and Jaume Llansana – built a hot air balloon which they called *Tramuntana*, a name chosen by the schoolchildren of Igualada, the adventurers' home town. Lladó designed the balloon and oversaw its construction; Comellas sewed together the nine hundred pieces which composed the balloon fabric; and Llansana cut nylon patches, wove the wicker basket – and chafed at the bit. When it was ready, the *Tramuntana* was shipped to Dar es Salaam and forwarded on to the island of Zanzibar, where the adventure was to begin, as had the novel. There too had begun the journeys of Burton, Livingstone and Stanley.

In the final trials the diesel-oil burner didn't work – or rather, it worked too well and they had to use a fire extinguisher on it. They plumped for propane gas instead – safer, if hard to obtain in Africa. A propane burner was sent out from London, while the adventurers waited on a desert island near Zanzibar, living like Robinson Crusoes in company with eighty giant tortoises. Llansana enhanced their chances of delay by being the first to succumb to malaria.

On 30th January 1980, *Tramuntana* made its first flight over the sea, the wind pushing it straight out towards India! Two hours' struggling to control altitude brought it back into line. A week later, after some uneventful flights to the west, the three put down heavily in a rice field and were tried for causing damage to the crop. Declared innocent, they proceeded, trying to avoid being shot for overflying a prohibited zone. Over Mzenga-Selous Game Reserve, two days later, they ran out of gas and had to undertake a two-day 110-km march across open country without food and with very little water. An attack by a wild boar kept them on their toes. Then they came to a village and collected an entourage, consisting of a policeman, a doctor, a teacher-cum-soldier and a Party official, all friendly and obliging. Thus escorted, they arrived at a larger town, where they were handed over – to the police. Set free, they discovered they had been robbed of $1,000. Suspect number one was the policeman.

Later, the Spaniards enjoyed a five-week spell at a campsite in Tanzania, where they gave free flights to tourists (one of which ended on a cabin roof) in return for food and the use of facilities.

The resumption of their progress westward coincided with a change of wind direction which necessitated flying at much greater height. From the air, elephants looked like beetles; vultures flew beneath the balloon basket. Landing on a mountain, clear of the game reserve at last and thinking they were safe, the crew were charged by a rhinoceros.

Towards the end of March, they suffered their first real mishap. Having been too lavish in their use of fuel, they ran out just as they were landing. The balloon wrapped itself around a tree and was torn in several places. Llansana got out of the basket with a twisted foot. Often, landing sites would appear deserted; the natives' inquisitiveness was surpassed by their nervousness and they would hide in the scrub until they were certain that the balloon was not a bomb visited upon them by an enemy power. The winds were uncooperative; a second uneven landing tore new holes in the fabric; and then Comellas went down with malaria.

Faced with these problems, Lladó nonetheless tried to make some progress on his own. It is difficult for just one person to inflate the balloon and (as Llansana commented) "even more so with the help of well-intentioned natives". He managed it, got aloft, and flew over the same village for the third time running. The natives didn't understand. "Don't you have aeroplanes in your country?" they asked, puzzled. By 2nd May, the team were anxious to put some more distance behind them and allowed Lladó another solo trip. In a catastrophic landing, however, he was thrown out of the basket and dragged along the ground until the balloon buried itself in some trees. The pilot was injured and there was no one nearby to help him. It took nine days to sew up the balloon.

They decided to call a halt to solo flights, though instead they sometimes flew at night when the winds were weaker and interfered less with the process of inflation. Lladó developed an interesting technique of deliberately hitting the top of a tree to reduce the balloon's speed – with very good results. Another thing he developed, on 30th May, was malaria: the trio was complete.

Gas, or lack of it, was a constant problem. On one occasion, the police themselves brought it to the team from a town 120 km distant. On another, a group of Africans was persuaded to mount a two-day cycling expedition to bring ten cylinders to the balloon site.

Bureaucracy, of the kind that encroached on them more and more as time went on, was a phenomenon beyond even Jules Verne's vision. The Spanish threesome was arrested for this and detained for that; visas expired; papers by the ream had to be produced. Unfortunately, boundaries do not exist in the air and the wind would take no notice of them if they did. When it came time to leave Tanzania, with the authorities now hot on their trail, a northerly wind blew them along parallel to the frontier, which remained a frustrating 200 metres away. They were heading for Burundi, where they were expected and for which they had all the required entry papers; but they didn't get there. In a long, swift flight they at last made it out of Tanzania – and into Rwanda, where they had no permission to fly and, in any case, lacked personal visas. Inevitably, they were directed to a military base. *Tramuntana* was 'expelled' from the country and taken to the Tanzanian frontier, its pilots being kept under constant surveillance as spies in the best thrillers always are. Four weeks of negotiations secured another round of permits. Flight number thirty took them straight as an arrow towards Uganda, a country occupied by three or four different 'armies' following the recent defeat of Idi Amin.

Not unnaturally, they were reluctant to cross the frontier in a brightly-coloured balloon which would make them sitting ducks. A landing was imperative. The balloon dragged and bounced along the ground, roughly spilling its passengers and their equipment along its bumpy route to an engagement with a huge, sharp-branched tree. A fight to the death between tree and balloon ensued. The tree won.

It took Llansana, Lladó and Comellas fifteen days to recuperate and rebuild the balloon before they could risk another flight. Airborne again, they soared as high as 6,300 metres. Only afterwards were they alerted to the danger of passing over the volcano Nyaragongo, where thermals rise to 20,000 metres.

In Zaïre, they were naturally taken for Belgian mercenaries and put in the hands of the military. A village chief demanded to see their papers authorising travel in the country – a meaningless formality, since he couldn't read. 'Rescued' by a corrupt political commissar, they flew on over the Virungas National Park to a landing in the village of Bambo, where the natives assumed that their arrival was a portent of the end of the world and greeted the travellers brandishing Bibles.

By the end of August, the balloonists began to suspect that the season of trade winds was over (at least at their usual flying altitudes). Tropical downpours began to occur with devastating unpredictability. Rough landings were the order of the day. Once, in thick jungle, they came down on top of the trees and descended to the ground inside the basket as if they were in a lift.

A few more flights in the National Park, with no particular destination or direction and no motive other than to enjoy themselves, and they called an end to the expedition.

In the words of Jules Verne's father: "Everything that man is capable of imagining will be realised by other men". Verne's imagined balloon flight across Africa was indeed, more or less, realised – even if it took 117 years to come to pass and ten times longer to complete in the air than in the mind.

UNDERWATER RISIBILITY

As the Diving Officer of the Aquaticus Diving School pointed out from his position of authority (under the table, having downed five pints at the weekly club meeting), the quickest way of climbing the ladder from Third Class to Second Class diver is to organise a successful club project.

F. Walton, Third Class, drawing on the same liquid inspiration as the D.O., swiftly bubbled up with a suggestion. After due, if not sober, consideration of the other proposals – among which the top contenders were (a) raising the Titanic, and (b) a quick collective grope with the local good-time girl – Walton's idea took the biscuit by default. This was: underwater hang-gliding.

Local pilots were approached in the hope that they'd loan the club a hang-glider; much advice was offered – some of it unprintable – but no-one seemed inclined to equip the project until a manufacturer, Skyhook Sailwings Ltd., was cornered and talked into parting with a brand new, high performance model.

So it was that in August 1981 the five founder members of the Aquaticus underwater hang gliding squadron set forth to make the first, and probably the last, test flight. They had chosen the blue pool, Llangollen, for its clear water, its depth (not more than 12 metres) and for certain safety reasons.

Ten diving sets, the hang glider, ropes, buoys and the club camera were lugged about 300 metres uphill. The equipment was then lowered down the side of the quarry, the glider rigged, surface supporting buoys attached to the release system and the divers kitted up. The ten-metre glider was manoeuvred into deep water, where she hung, said Walton, "looking for all the world like a ghostly giant manta ray".

Two metres underwater, Walton hung in his harness waiting to be released from the buoys. Heart and breathing apparatus in mouth, he gave the signal. Would he plummet straight to the bottom and be smothered?, he wondered. Would the descent be too rapid for him to clear his ears? How does a high performance machine perform when low?

Six months of planning and preparation proved their worth. Walton found himself moving gracefully forward and down at the gentlest of angles and speeds. When the bottom came in sight, he pushed the control bar out, slowed down to a stop and stood up to make a perfect landing.

To celebrate this remarkable triumph, the Diving School held an underwater barbecue at which smoke reduced visibility to nil.

READY, WILLIG AND ABE

In the World Trade Center's archives, this story is classified under 'Publicity – Demonstrations or Exhibitions – Unauthorised'. Since unauthorised exhibitions at Manhattan's tallest building never fail to attract frenzied publicity of the kind that authorised events have to sweat and slave for, this must be a pretty fat file. A damage suit for 'services, costs and expenses' was brought after the unauthorised exploit in question: 'To wit: intentionally, wilfully and wrongfully scaling and climbing the South Tower of the World Trade Center.'

The year was 1977 and the villain was George Willig, then 27, a trained horticulturalist, professional toy designer and amateur mountaineer who had climbed '30 or 40 mountains' in the previous four years. A quiet and modest man with no axe to grind, no overpowering ambition and no obvious psychological hang-ups, Willig planned the climb for one Wednesday in May but then remembered that he had an appointment as a blood donor and so put the climb off for a day. Starting at about 6.30 am, he got about three metres off the ground before he was first spotted, by a window cleaner.

The key to the ascent was a T-shaped device which he designed himself to lock into the finger-width grooves that run up the corner of each tower. The grooves, about a hundred cms. apart, are normally used to support scaffolding for the window cleaners. From a chest harness, a rope ran through a ring to each foot. Willig used the jumaring principle of putting his weight on one foot, then sliding the grip up the groove to take his weight on the other foot while the device was moved up again. When he wasn't resting, he was able to climb at the rate of a storey a minute. 'It was like climbing up a ladder', he said afterwards.

Willig was well on his way up the sheer 412-metre face of the tower when a policeman and a Port Authority patrolman pulled alongside in a motorised scaffold. Police Officer DeWitt Allen greeted Willig with: "We've got to stop meeting like this. My wife is getting suspicious". Asked if he'd like to join them in the bucket, Willig, who had moved from one groove to another so as to be out of their reach, said politely "No, I'd like to climb to the top". Chatting amiably, signing autographs for his 'co-ascenders' and chewing his cinnamon bread and honey snacks, Willig proceeded coolly on his way. Having reached the top at 10.05 am, he pulled himself through a 75-cm-wide hatchway to the roof and turned to wave to the thunderously applauding crowd below.

Needless to say, he was then arrested and charged with criminal trespass, reckless endangerment and disorderly conduct. A sum of $250,000 mentioned in connection with the initial charges, to cover traffic and crowd control, came down at about the same speed as the World Trade Center's express elevators. According to a police spokesman, a quick audit had revealed that the total cost to the Center and the city – manpower, overtime and fuel for the police helicopter included – had been $2,403.18. Within a day, a generous Mayor Abe Beame had settled out of court for $1.10 – one cent for each storey climbed – and a promise from the miscreant, whose 'tremendous courage' he praised, to consult with World Trade Center engineers on ways of preventing future attempts to climb the towers.

The 'human fly' became an instant, somewhat reluctant, celebrity. Like Philippe Petit, who walked the high wire between the towers of the Center in 1974, George Willig claimed there was "nothing I really wanted. I'm a climber", he said. "I like to climb. It was another climb." Inevitably, the media wouldn't let it go at that. What kind of stunt was he planning next?, people wanted to know. "I haven't thought of an encore" was his reply. "I'm not in show business". There are those who would give him an argument about that.

DALY OF DELIGHT

Now come all ye sports that want a lot of fun,
Roll up your swag and pack up a gun,
Get a bit of flour, sugar and tea,
Don't forget a gallon of gool old O.P.*,
Crank up your lizzie and come along with me,
And I'll show you sights as you never did see,
Down on the Daly River-O! . . .

*rum   41

A later verse of the old song tells of 'Wallaby George, Charlie Dargie, Old Slim Davis, Jimmy Panquee, Big Mouth Charlie and old Porce, the Tipperary Pong and Jim Wilkie' – a band of men not dissimilar from Warwick Deacock, Laurie Jeays and four of their pals, modern versions of the old colonials, who met together to splash down the Daly River from Katherine, 240 km south of Darwin, in Australia's Northern Territory, to wherever they ended up. It was a bit of an impulse, suitable for wanderers with a little spare time and a lot of curiosity.

Jeays from Brisbane first had the idea. A boat builder and carpenter by trade, he had a romantic bent that had never got straightened out. He was good at straightening out nails, though: he'd learned that as a child from his Anzac father. So Laurie was just the chap to improvise two prototype five-metre galvanised iron canoes – cheap, instant, and disposable to boot. He announced in a one-page letter that the trip was on, and anyone who wanted to be part of it should be at Katherine at 9.30 am on a certain day in July. There were Ron and also Fritz, an Austrian, who came down from Darwin. Jim and guitar headed north from Kangaroo Valley in New South Wales. Warwick, who lives in Sydney, dropped by on his way back from Portuguese Timor, bringing three Chinese-made aluminium billy cans he'd bought there and a bottle of Portuguese brandy. Laurie, with his mate Peter, turned up from Brisbane, with a plan on the back of an envelope, disposable tools and oddments of gear.

It took from 10 am to 5 pm to put the canoes together. They looked alright, so the crew, balancing on what seemed a mountain of gear, and wielding makeshift paddles of waterproof plywood, splashed off to find camp for the night. Fritz was relieved to stop. He'd never been in a canoe before, not even a real one, and was having trouble 'finding his seat'.

That night they huddled under a patent plastic fly with mosquito net all round, surrounded by booby traps trip-wired with shotgun cartridges for protection against man-eating crocodiles. Then they discovered that there are no mosquitoes in those parts and that the crocodiles so far inland are fish-eaters and man-shy anyway, so later on they just built a fire in a trough in the sand.

They learned something else the next day when Deacock hit rocks in a rapid, sank his canoe with all hands and some film, and creased his knee on the gunwale. From then on they got out in advance of rapids to have a look, sledged the craft down tricky stretches on the end of ropes and often swam alongside or behind (holding on to dodge under pandanus branches).

Half rations were supplemented with freshly-caught barramundi fish cooked in butter. Next to Jim's guitar, sitting in the bow of a canoe, was a gun which someone had brought along for no particular reason. Some of the party thought of it vaguely in connection with rampaging water buffalo, but these turned out, like the killer crocs, to live further north in Arnhemland. It wasn't meant for sport shooting – none of them would have dreamed of harming the inquisitive wallabies, charmers all. But Laurie found a use for the gun when he ran full tilt into a wild pig on the other side of a bush. A warning shot sent her off, but not before Laurie had got an unpleasantly detailed close-up of her tusks. He came down the river bank fast, and for a time they had four tiny piglets on their hands.

Later on they nearly collected bullets themselves when a stockman out hunting dogmeat with some aboriginals mistook them for kangaroos – until they leapt up and down, yelling, to prove how human they were. They got some salt beef out of the encounter, and a drop of 'corrugated milk', as the stockman called his rum.

No hour was dull, no two days similar. It was sometimes hard and often exciting and there was plenty to learn about each other over the nightly campfires. Peter himself unwound over his fishing rod. Jim strummed his guitar and composed songs featuring their disposable floating homes, now called 'Blackjack' and 'Gravel Grinder'.

None of the really nasty things they'd been told about – by those who never go – happened. Apart from the near-misses with the pig and the stockman, the worst they could manage was a thoroughly good all-over itch from tiny red kangaroo ticks, picked up in an idyllic pool full of white and purple water lilies.

There are two kinds of places in that area: those that are shown on a map and don't exist – like peanut farms and old homesteads; and those that are hard to find on the map but are there on the ground. Colloo Crossing is one of the latter. There, nearly 500 km and twelve days after starting, they called halt and gave their canoes to a farmer's son.

That was in 1969.

But the river stayed in the back of Warwick Deacock's mind and in 1979 he went back for another look. Laurie Jeays went along too and this time suggested packing cases for transport. He made two 2.4 x 1.2 metre boxes, filled them with gear and sent them by road to Katherine, where the river travellers were again to meet. Using the packing cases, they knocked together some punts measuring 3.7 x 1.2 and 5 x 1.2 metres, two sets of oars and a few paddles, found an old grill on a rubbish tip and loaded in some jam tins, rations and fishing lines. Then they pushed the two toughest young men into the punts and ordered them to row.

Row they did, heartily if not merrily, for an hour. The result wasn't good. The river flow near Katherine is about two knots; they made three. Since they couldn't beat the river, they decided, happily enough, to join it. They put away their maps and let time, the environment and the river take care of the trip. They observed some changes; the crocodiles were distributed differently, the aboriginals had moved away; the river banks had been burned off. All the same, they agreed that to travel the

Daly in boxes was the best of all package holidays.

Formidable Feet

"I'm an amateur inventor and I've been working on water shores for four years. Ever since Jesus Christ walked on water, man has been trying to prove he can do the same on a liquid surface".

So said Sergeant Walter Robinson, then 31, an American soldier stationed at Karlsruhe, West Germany, in August 1978.

And indeed Sgt Robinson became the first person to walk the English Channel. He set off from Shakespeare Beach, near Dover, and reached Cap Gris Nez, on the French coast, 11½ hours later, in good conditions.

Walked? Sort of. The 2.4-metre-long 'water shoe' on which Robinson stood looked like a cross between a snowshoe and a surfboard. He used two long oars for propulsion.

A formidable feat, but not perhaps what you and I would call walking. Will the real Jesus Christ please stand up?

"ALL GOES IF COURAGE GOES"

"They have just accomplished the sort of feat of which the British are fond but which, it must be said, does not arouse the same excitement on this side of the Channel."
Thus the newspaper *La Voix du Nord*, Lille, on 2nd September 1980.

In a way the laconic correspondent was right. The French variety of excitement aroused was indeed different from the British. In Sangatte, near Calais, it took the form of an alarmed farmer waving a double-barrelled shotgun and complaining to the police that foreigners were burning fiery crosses in his field. Next, the gendarmerie carted off to the police station a group of Britons whose method of entry into France must have seemed decidedly eccentric. Here, charges were mentioned of violating French air space, trespassing and failure to obtain immigration and Customs clearance. The British consular representative was summoned from his bed to vouch for the charitable nature of the British exploit. Meanwhile, bootloads of beer were carried from British cars and distributed amongst the gendarmerie to promote a spirit of goodwill.

Communications had failed, as they often do. Clearance had been obtained from the French immigration authorities but local gendarmes had not been informed. But why all the fuss? Mainly because of the unusual manner of the intruders' arrival. A team of six servicemen had just made the first ever parachute descent across the Channel.

Exercise Courage '80, as it was nicknamed, was sponsored by Courage Breweries to the tune of £8,000. Through sponsorship at so much per man per mile, together with a competition, the team raised about £50,000 for the Association for Spina Bifida and Hydrocephalus. The six jumpers were led by 43-year-old Warrant Officer II Ted Lewington (now owner of a parachute training school), who for the previous twelve years had been responsible for the famous freefall parachute team, the Red Devils. The jump took place in the early hours of 31st August 1980, starting from a Piper Navajo aircraft, at about 7,625 metres above Dover Castle, Kent.

The parachutists wore thermal clothing, RAF immersion suits, lifejackets, boots, balaclavas and gloves, and carried specially designed oxygen packs and radios (only two of these, however, were found to be working during the descent). The British-made rectangular aerodynamic parachutes, known as 'flying mattresses', had a failsafe mechanism – the Irvin Hitefinder – fitted to the reserves and set to fire at 1,525 metres above sea level, unless disarmed, a process each member had to perform once his main chute was fully open.

Air traffic controllers in four countries stood by to clear a 1.6-km-wide corridor of all aircraft at the time of the descent. A Wessex helicopter, the Red Devils' own Islander and a patrol boat all maintained a watch on the team.

The record attempt was originally set for 1st June but the weather wouldn't come right. Day in, day out, at 12 noon, a representative of the team telephoned the Met. Office to ascertain the forecast. Time began grow short, as did the days. Strictly, three weather elements were identified as constituting adequate conditions for the jump: a north to northwest wind blowing at 60 knots at 7,625 m; a twenty knot (or thereabouts) wind from about 915 metres; and a maximum of two-eighths cloud cover. It was a less practical factor which prompted the team to fall into place as soon as possible: competition. A German team was just a step behind them in their preparations.

Having been given a favourable weather report, the British group assembled at RAF Manston, Kent, to board their plane. Then from the Met. Office came disappointing news of veering and increasing winds and a gale warning in one area. Lewington screwed his Courage to the sticking point and decided they'd go ahead. RAF computers could offset the place at which they would jump from the aircraft to compensate for the severe weather conditions. They went.

For the first six seconds the team freefell, then opened their chutes smartly at 7,320 metres. The French coast was immediately visible, though it seemed a very long way off. The team maintained excellent formation, travelling at about 95 kmph, and crossed the French coast at heights of between 2,745 and 915 metres, where the ground staff – but not the farmers or police – were in readiness. Each parachutist chose his own landing spot and was recovered by the Wessex to be transported to the designated dropping and (unfriendly-)reception zone at Sangatte.

By covering the 33.6 km from Dover to Sangatte in 26 minutes, 22 seconds, the team also secured a second record: the fastest Channel crossing other than by a powered aircraft. Everyone was jubilant, not least about having won a British 'first'. "The Germans might have chased us out of Dunkirk," crowed their pilot, "but we beat them to Calais in the air".

Taste for Adventure

Altitude has a peculiar effect on climbers' tastes and aversions in food. Writing in John Hunt's *The Ascent of Everest**, Griffith Pugh and George Band noted laconically that "High up on Everest in 1933 [Eric] Shipton had a craving for a dozen eggs; [Frank] Smythe wanted frankfurters and sauerkraut; in 1924 [Howard] Somervell's favourite diet was strawberry jam and condensed milk; on Gho Oyu [Edmund] Hillary wanted pineapple cubes and [Cam] Secord wanted tinned salmon. In general, men prefer to eat nothing rather than put up with something that is distasteful to them..."

*Hodder & Stoughton, 1953. Appendix VI, Diet.

Sailing Through Paris

Christian Nau of Paris has been a landyachting enthusiast since he was ten years old. Piloting a modern version of one of these ancient vehicles – which date back almost as far as the wheel – he has crossed the Sahara three times, inaugurated a section of the Paris-Brussels motorway, trundled around the islands of Réunion and Kerguelen (49°S) and in April 1971 traversed Paris. On that occasion, Nau, wearing a lounge suit, wove his landyacht in and out among the Renaults and Citroëns from the Esplanade des Invalides to the Place de la Concorde. He circumnavigated the Luxor Obelisk seven times to allow photographers to immortalise his exploit and the international press duly made a fuss of him and his vehicle, *Nouakchott* (vintage Sahara 1967). The Parisian public, however, did little more than cast him a slightly disconcerted glance and applaud his adoption of a means of transport that would use air without abusing it.

TRY ANYTHING ONCE

Then turn not pale, beloved snail,
but come and join the dance.
> – Lewis Carroll, *Alice in Wonderland.*

WILD THING ONE

It was in about 1970 that the sport of hoverbogganing was invented. It was a few minutes afterwards that the sport died a sudden death.

The hoverboggan in question was the first ever built, and probably the only one. Made by some workers at an agricultural engineering factory near Wallingford, Oxfordshire, it consisted almost solely of one of the large steel-framed pallets upon which engineering components were stacked. A fan, operated by a small lawn-mower motor, forced a flow of air under the frame and base of the pallet. With this device, one man could easily shift several tons of machinery.

It occurred to the factory workers that the rolling slopes of the Thames Valley would provide a superb setting for their new sport. They managed to get Wild Thing One, as they called the hoverpallet, onto a trailer and towed the lot onto a farmer's field. One side of this descended in easy stages to a gentle run out onto a meadow by the placid Thames. The other side of the pasture was a steeper slope, traversed by barbed wire, beyond which grazed a herd of cows. The breeze seemed so gentle that the sportsmen ignored its direction, which was towards the steep slope, the wire and the cows.

A smart pull on the cord and the motor started. Four or five men jumped on and sat so that their weight was evenly distributed. They had taken the precaution of tethering the pallet to a stake in the ground to forestall the premature launch of Wild Thing One.

The peg was yanked out. With surprising rapidity, the hoverboggan gathered speed. The ground was fairly smooth but even so the frame wobbled so much that its corners touched the ground, making the pallet veer alarmingly. The breeze continued to exert its gentle pressure. Inexorably, Wild Thing One drifted over the field's high point, still accelerating, and shot down towards the startled cows.

No-one thought to cut the motor; or perhaps the idea was rejected for fear of provoking a ground loop, since the chances of surviving at 50 kmph would have been slim. With a whiplash crack they tore through the barbed wire, hurtled through the herd and spun out onto marshy ground. Here they cut the motor and jumped clear while Wild Thing One bogged down in the soggy terrain. They got it out, after a long struggle. But they didn't pursue the sport of hoverbogganing. Wild Thing Once was enough.

HOW BRAZILIAN BALLOONING WENT LIKE A BOMB

Robert J. Rechs, of California, tells this story of how he was invited to introduce ballooning to Brazil in November 1970:

"I have travelled quite a bit in Latin countries, so when a wealthy South American industrialist invited me to build him a sport balloon, I never expected the offer to be followed up. I knew a bit about the *mañana* philosophy. But one day after months of correspondence, a messenger knocked at my door, asked my name and promptly counted a pile of hundred-dollar bills into my hand, then concluded by putting an airline ticket on top.

At that point, I gathered that I had a serious proposition and set about buying hardware and fabric for the construction of a balloon. Knowing how even little misunderstandings can swamp the best-planned projects, I telephoned my benefactor the day before I left and asked him to clarify certain points. The main one was: "Do you have pure quality propane available in Brazil?". "Of course," he replied, with a detectable tone of disgust, "Propagas, made in Brazil, is the best in the world". Not wanting to insult him further, I took him at his word.

Two days later I stood in front of São Paulo airport wondering why so many people were enthusiastically waving and shouting as though they'd never seen anyone get off an aeroplane before. My strange-looking equipment and I breezed through Customs and came out into the crowd, all of whom wanted to kiss me or shake my hand as I was escorted to a big black limousine.

"Well," I thought, "if this is the way they treat balloonists here, I know I'm going to like this". I was met by my host, driven to a beautiful country villa about forty km west of the city and given a splendid meal at a festively decorated table. Over apéritifs on the verandah, we toasted 'the new balloon' and my host assured me that all the facilities in the country, and of course his own personal facilities, were at my disposal to ensure that the project reached fruition.

The status and influence of my benefactor was slowly dawning on me. Together we visited a large industrial complex, with his name prominently displayed. Even the tone of the machinery seemed respectfully muted. The workers wore brand new 'coveralls' but their feet were bare, despite the fact that the floor was strewn with sharp metal chips, mixed liberally with plating acids. "You wouldn't want them to ruin their valuable shoes, would you?" my guide asked by way of explanation.

During the tour of inspection, as we stood in a large production area crowded with about a hundred employees, my host enquired what sort of space I would need for the construction of the balloon. "Oh, a room about half this size" I replied. Click! went his fingers and all the workers promptly stood up, lifted the work benches and, squeezing into half the area they had occupied before, carried on working as though this sort of rearrangement occurred daily. My slightest wish was apparently a command.

With cooperation like that, it wasn't surprising that within two weeks we had a beautiful new balloon. Constant anxious enquiries had accompanied its manufacture; now the day came for the test inflation, bright and sunny. Strange: besides the bird song, I could also detect a muted vibration in the air. I peeked out of my window and saw maybe a hundred well-dressed people sipping wine from crystal glasses, speaking in hushed tones and moving about sedately. Obviously a grand occasion of some sort. Well then, why hadn't I been invited? I jumped into my clothes and went out the back door to mingle with the guests. As I walked around, the crowd parted for me and started to applaud.

In the middle of the gathering was my host, dressed in the finest astronaut suit you'd ever see (and *then* only in a space travel museum). At any other ballooning event I should just have collapsed with laughter, but something told me this was a solemn occasion. Besides, my host had obviously spent lavishly to make the event a success. After I'd been briefly presented to the guests and after another toast to the new balloon, I was introduced to my eager ground crew. They were:

the Commanding General of the Army,
the Commanding General of the Air Force,
the Commander of the Navy,
the Honourable Director of Civil Aviation,
the Governor of the State of São Paulo,
and others; the list went on and on.

At this point, I began to feel a little uneasy. The day

had been designated for a simple test only, not the grand finale. Never mind, I said to myself, what can possibly go wrong after so much assiduous preparation? So I briefed the attentive ground crew thoroughly and got everybody into his place. Then I lit the pilot light and pulled the 'blast' valve.

Pssssst. The flame went out.

Every eye was riveted on me; but the observers remained undaunted; they seemed to assume that I knew what I was doing. I relit the pilot light and pulled the handle again.

Pssssst.

This time the faces turned sour. My astronaut-host now rushed up to me, feathers flying, and enquired in a whisper what the problem might be. I didn't return the favour of confidentiality but asked out loud, in a voice everyone could hear:

"Are you sure this fuel is propane?"

To the crowd circling around me, this was an insult. To judge from their faces, I might as well have been dancing on the Brazilian flag. Fingers pointed to the label on the fuel bottle, which read: 'Propane, another fine product of Brazil'.

I tried several more times to light the flame but with the same result. At length I stiffened my resolve and repeated my accusation.

"This is NOT propane and, whatever it is, it is no good in a balloon".

That did it. The crew downed tools, strode to their chauffeured cars and disappeared in a cloud of dust. The crowd dispersed. Within seconds, I was standing all alone with the balloon. I went back to bed, pulled the covers over my head and went to sleep, hoping it was all a bad dream. It wasn't. When I rose again, I discovered that even the servants were shunning me. I'd had no breakfast and there appeared to be a distinct danger that lunch wouldn't be forthcoming either. Hunger was obviously going to drive me to find a solution rather smartly. I returned to the factory nonchalantly, but it was apparent that every employee already knew that the incompetent American had caused the company to lose face. I found a telephone directory and dialled the Propagas company. They found me an English-speaking engineer.

"This Propagas of yours," I said to him, "what exactly is its chemical name?"

"Why," he replied, "butane, of course. We don't produce propane in Brazil – it's more expensive. Besides, since it's a price-controlled item, we dilute the butane by twenty per cent to allow ourselves a fair profit".

"Why do you call it Propagas then?" I asked, bewildered.

"It's a better-sounding trade name" was his reply.

I got his name for reference, thanked him and rang off. Then I went and made myself a cup of coffee, marched with it right into my benefactor's office, sat down and put my feet up on his polished desk. His face went from pale to livid.

"I found your problem" I said. "Propagas is low-vapour pressure butane mixed with twenty per cent water. The Brazilian people only use it for cooking and don't know that they're being cheated on their only source of gas".

I handed him the 'phone number of my Propagas informant and sauntered away again. "Call me when you get the business resolved".

After that, it didn't take long for the whole of Brazil to spring into action, reaction and overreaction. The news was passed on to the Commanding General of the Army. The gas company was shut down, the director fired, and within the hour my friendly engineer was standing in front of me, begging me to spare him from a fate worse than death! By 8 am the following morning we held South America's entire propane supply. Another 2,250 litres were promised us within ten days.

And what a difference this simple item made! The balloon now inflated as it was supposed to and produced the much delayed excitement. Adults, children and dogs all took off in terror as the balloon made its first ascent, with me and my local astronaut aboard. Cars careered off the road, hysteria reigned.

I didn't care: it was a magnificent flight, in the early morning sun. Soon we found ourselves approaching a picturesque little colonial village called Cotia, so I descended to about 60 metres over the roof-tops for a closer look. When the first head popped out and looked up with a panic-stricken expression, I began to wonder whether I'd been unwise to go in so close. In less than a minute, there was pandemonium: shouting, screaming and then gunshots. I was out of there like a flash, climbing for my life.

We went on, enjoying the flight and forgetting the recent dangers, until the time came to land. Wishing to avoid 'hostile' territory, I picked a field ahead as a landing place, skimmed the tree tops, made a three-point landing and looked around. We were not alone. The field turned out to be a rural schoolyard and in it, behind a fence, cowered a thousand or more schoolchildren and teachers, motionless with fright.

My astronaut benefactor, equal to the occasion, saved the day by becoming a bit of a showman. Standing on top of the basket, he loudly proclaimed himself to be Santa Claus. Bang! Down went the fences and the crowd surged towards us, trampling everything. Not even our lovely new balloon was spared.

Leaving servants to collect the pieces of balloon, we returned to the villa by chauffeured car, by way of Cotia, which was in an extraordinary state of commotion. There was an unbelievable traffic jam; it looked almost as though civil war had broken out and the city were being evacuated. Armed police and mean-looking militiamen were everywhere. Still, they snapped to attention when they saw us – all big black chauffeured cars are considered important – so we passed on, unhindered and a bit smug. It had been a fruitful flight, well worthy of the celebration feast with which the day ended.

On the way to the airport next day, I noticed a picture of our balloon, on the front page of a São Paulo newspaper. I don't read Portuguese, so I got a bystander to translate the banner headlines:

'TERRORISTS DROP BOMB OVER COTIA FROM A STRANGE AIRCRAFT'!"

Ah yes, Brazil, where the nuts come from.

Salisbury Plane

At the time of planning his flight by microlight aircraft from Salisbury, England, to Salisbury (now Harare) Zimbabwe, Philip Berent, an English economics student, was unabashed about justifying the venture in political terms. "I thought of the . . . flight" he said "because I like what is happening in Zimbabwe politically: the change from white supremacy to majority rule". By the time he was ready to set out on his 23,200-km flight (early 1983), the capital of Zimbabwe had changed its name and the political situation in the country had changed from black-and-white to colour (particularly splashes of red). The adventurer approached for sponsorship a truck manufacturer, 'the makers of drinks, TVs, cigarettes and maybe Durex'. Reporting this, *The Guardian* newspaper added engagingly: 'He'd even consider a condominium'. (Condom-inium? With Durex?).

MAKE STRAIGHT IN THE DESERT A HIGHWAY . . .

When, to silence an over-talkative friend in a turkish bath, Richard Slowe floated the idea of taking his fort-night's summer holiday in the form of an independent African adventure-safari, even he didn't believe it. As a conversation-stopper the suggestion had its merits, but out in the cold light of day it looked pretty bleak. Or so he thought, until he began to study maps, take advice and allow imagination, plus what he called 'pride and stupidity', to prevail. The plan was to drive across the Sahara.

Three companions threw in their lot with him, hope triumphing over inexperience. All four were aged between 21 and 23, Jews from fairly affluent families, well educated, cultured, civilised, full of *savoir vivre* and humour, and ignorant to the nth degree about travel outside Europe. One, Howard Cohen, was an expert amateur mechanic, but that was the sum total of their qualifications for the journey. They soon acquired four faulty and ancient Land-Rovers which, by processes of prestidigitation and transplant surgery, they transformed into two serviceable, if still ancient, vehicles, selling off the remains of the others at a respectable price by perhaps somewhat less than respectable means. All their hopes were now pinned on the two survivors, which they named Fred and Charlie. With these they would drive across Europe, sail to Africa, climb the Atlas mountains, cross the Sahara to 'Black Africa', follow the River Niger, and finally turn south to Lagos on the Gulf of Guinea. Simple! In Nigeria, a friend would sell their vehicles for them and they would fly home. With sanguine optimism, they booked the homeward flight.

As they were to travel in Arab lands, the fact of being Jewish gave them pause. Cohen considered passing himself off as Mohammed for the duration, but they decided – and found in the end – that this was the least of their problems.

Their preparations did little to enhance their expertise and less to boost their confidence. After all, as Slowe wondered, "How do you practise going across a desert? Drive along Margate beach trying to avoid the sandcastles?" With fists full of documents, rears full of injections and hearts full of optimism, they set off, in as much English-gentleman style as they could muster, one Tuesday in September 1969.

Even before they reached the coast, Charlie began to leak oil, not for the last time. Refusing to admit that this constituted a major disaster, the group decided to ignore the fault and drive on until the vehicle simply wouldn't go any further. Charlie rewarded their faith and kept going for some 1,500 km before the oil seal received the attentions of an enthusiastic mechanic in Spain.

In Algeria they drove head-on into one of the major problems of their trip. Unwittingly they carried with them the spice of other British people's ineptitude to add variety to the indigestible fare of bureaucratic hassles and cultural oddities which was served up to them throughout Africa. For example: "The tourist discount vouchers [for petrol] which we had been told we could buy at the Algerian border could now be purchased only through banks in the main towns, and we were officially advised that Colomb-Béchar was the one place on the route which we were taking where the vouchers would be available. Several days and many hundreds of miles later, when we arrived at Colomb-Béchar, we were to learn from an amused bank official that vouchers could be purchased only at the border".* Just as bad was the fact that a British insurance broker 'specialising in African policies' had sold them vehicle insurance that

*Richard Slowe: *Innocents in Africa*. Royal Automobile Club, London, 1979.

was invalid in Africa; state insurance had to be bought for cash at an exorbitant price.

Inquisitive callers at their overnight camps were sent packing with gifts of cigarettes, for which they appeared profoundly grateful, thanking the travellers profusely in Arabic and smilingly adding what was evidently the only foreign phrase they knew. "Heil Hitler!" they said, and waited for applause.

The quartet got on well together despite constant mishaps, of which burst pneumatic tent tubes, collapsing collapsible lavatories and wet plugs were but a few. Francis Norton, who had elected to be cook and camp orderly, for want of any other useful qualification, regularly made them ill with his cooking. And Charlie the Land-Rover went from worse to worst. By the time they reached Colomb-Béchar Richard Slowe, who was driving the vehicle, realised that Charlie was already, to put it bluntly, a write-off. However, making the unilateral decision that the journey should not be aborted, he kept the truth from the others and they pressed on. Like a man obsessed, Slowe "drove three good friends into the middle of the Sahara Desert relying upon my judgement" (which was to fail them) "and a vehicle too sick to support them".

They reached Adrar, where they were to join a convoy for the crossing of the desert proper. The *Sub-Préfet* of the District granted them permission to proceed and waived an inspection of the vehicles on the grounds that 'Land-Rovers never go wrong'. Slowe breathed again. At the post office in Adrar they despatched what they thought was a witty cable home saying 'All's well and don't bother to send the balaclavas'. By the time it had passed through the butter-fingered hands of several telegraphic operators it read (or so the story went) 'Paul's well but his brother has eaten a barracuda'. Startled families back in England considered even this communication better than none.

Then the starting-point of the convoy was switched, with the minimum of notice, from Adrar to Reggane, some 142 km further south. The party made tracks – which they lost and found again. By now they had been joined by a French monk attached to a monastery in Togo. Jacques Fredouille had been on holiday in France and was driving back in his Citroën Deux-Chevaux. Their average speed during this section of the trip was a soaring 8 kmph, and they were often forced to use one or even two vehicles to drag another out of soft sand. In time they came to Reggane, the last inhabited oasis on the northern side of the Sahara, a town which, Slowe said, differs from Adrar, in that "whilst the archways in Adrar lead to the slums those in Reggane go nowhere".

The 'guides' they were offered to lead the convoy from Reggane onwards were an assorted bunch of Arabs travelling in an open-backed and rather battered Peugeot. With this vehicle in front, Fred driven by Richard Slotover with Cohen as navigator, Jacques in his 2CV and Slowe and Norton in Charlie bringing up the rear, the 'troupe of jokers' set out on their journey of 1,360 km. The guides galumphed off at about 80 kmph and halfway through the night managed to lose the rest of the convoy.

Charlie chose almost the same moment to expire. Oil had been slithering through the rear oil seal ever since they had left Hendon, the patch-up job in Spain having afforded only a temporary respite, and now it flowed in great waves through the clutch. Then the bearings gave out and the vehicle shuddered and sank to a standstill. Without quite knowing why, the travellers decided to take Charlie in tow. A splendid daybreak brought unbroken vistas of desert on all sides but no immediate trace of tracks, until Howard Cohen, scouting around, found a trail that led in approximately the right direction. This they decided to follow. Towing Charlie, however, was proving an intolerable burden on the ailing Fred, whose radiator was overheating constantly, despite frequent stops. If they went on, Fred would be burnt out and their precious water boiled away for nothing. Norton recorded their situation in his log:

" . . . 11.45 am *Position*: Hopeless – 130 miles south of Reggane and 265 miles north of Bordj-Perez (est.)
Temperature: 135⁰Fahrenheit, 57⁰ Centigrade (shade).
Remarks: Guide lost, Charlie dead, Fred limping and chances slim. Will the finder of these notes please send my love to mother."

It was clear that Charlie had to be dumped, together with half of their equipment. Out went Slowe's bed and two mattresses, a map-board, the spare tent and the stools, three empty jerrycans, all the extra paraffin, a vast quantity of surplus toilet paper, the picnic table – with which they had struggled to maintain the image of proper English gentlemen – and toothbrushes. They kept the portable lavatory.

Setting a match to a paraffin-drenched Charlie, they stood back and watched fifty per cent of their chance of crossing the desert go up in flames.

Three saddened Englishmen now piled into the remaining Land-Rover; Jacques had offered to take one passenger in his Citroën. Fred having "suffered rejection symptons when Howard transplanted the deceased's speedometer", the party was now without the means of recording their speed or distance but had to rely on prewar maps and their "accompanying monk's trust in God". With discomfort and inconvenience adding to their general state of desperation, they struggled onwards. Now their survival skills, such as they were, would be put to the supreme test.

The message of hope from above that day was transmitted to them through a sign in the wilderness. It read: 'Tropique du Cancer'. At last they had a tangible sign that they were heading the right way. Around six o'clock luck paid them another visit: they caught sight of their Arab guides. The Arabs' truck was so firmly swamped in soft sand that they had been forced to wait. It was less than encouraging for the Englishmen to learn that the guides had had to rewire their vehicle completely during the day, had lost power and had suffered two punctures.

It was a much chastened and only marginally wiser little group that continued south, reaching Bordj-Perez on the morning of the twelfth day out of Hendon. From here on, there was a road to follow which led to Tessalit, the frontier post with Mali, and the edge of 'Black Africa'.

The problems became increasingly difficult: with Fred's technical deficiencies, high humidity, mud tracks and wadis and quagmires from which they had to dig out the stranded vehicle with their one remaining spade and six empty Nesquik tins.

It was while they were attempting to make a dash to the River Niger that Jacques' vehicle hit a rock. The Citroën engine was pushed back with such force as to land almost in his lap. There was nothing for it but to abandon the vehicle. Two down, one to go. On they drove.

On the way to Goa, whence he was to fly back to Togo, Jacques delivered to his captive audience a lecture on the disposition and handling of the 'tin-god' – any minor African official whose sole joy lay in making the most of his ration of authority. It was a lesson that stood them in good stead – when, for example, on crossing into Dahomey, they were forced to complete three times and in triplicate, forms which required the ultimate in far-fetched detail. "Once again my dear grandmother's maiden name was being bandied about like so much hot news," wrote Slowe, "and although the publicity would have amused her I am sure she would have collapsed in a cold faint if she had known the number of times that her age had also been revealed".

The foursome found it easier to deal with the ordinary people of the countries through which they passed. Exchanges and barters were arranged to everyone's entertainment and satisfaction, petrol being paid for in kind on at least two occasions, once with two tins of stew, some washing-up liquid and two bars of soap, and another time with surplus jerrycans. Preparatory to the final run for home, they held a kind of downmarket garage sale in a village in Benin, selling off everything which was too heavy to be flown back to England, including more toilet paper, tinned meat, torches, sauce-pans, sleeping bags and a golfing umbrella.

Neither travelling difficulties nor political ones let up in any way. There were blind dashes across shared road-rail bridges (the driver would pray that the sharing might occur consecutively, not simultaneously); Francis in a moment of overconfidence knocked a passing rider off his bicycle, and continued to do his bit for his companions' loss of appetite; and the merry-go-round of petty official-dom offered repeated spins and spills.

Nigeria in 1969 was in the middle of the Biafran uprising and no place for foreigners, even those armed with nothing more than a mess tin, and its government did its best to deter the travellers from entering, staying or leaving, in that order or any other. In the end they were allowed to proceed to Lagos airport under escort of an ambulance. This afforded a unique source of delight by running out of petrol and having to be towed by its 'prisoners' to a town where the driver could sheepishly requisition a few litres of petrol.

Cohen, Slowe, Slotover and Norton caught their plane. Fate was obviously on their side after all. At the final desk they were presented with yet another form to complete. In answer to the question as to when they expected to return to Nigeria, they each independently wrote 'never'.

Charging through Africa, ever mindful of a time schedule, as Slowe and his companions did, is no way to become acquainted with the continent. And they knew it. On the rare occasions towards the end of their journey, when they had some time on their hands, they began to appreciate what they were having to miss. On the other hand, they experienced life to its limits, once or twice coming very near to stepping over into the alternative. And that is more than most of us get, even in a month of Sabbaths.

Blue Coats Over the White Cliffs of Dover

The famous white cliffs of England's southeast coast have been largely left alone by climbers, mainly because the chalk is loose and unstable. Early in 1981, Mick Fowler, Andy Meyers and Chris Watts, equipped with ice-screws, ice-axes, crampons and padded gloves, decided to set the record to rights. The ascent, interesting if fairly straightforward in itself, attracted the attention of the Coastguard, who, up to about the halfway mark, urged the climbers to come down and thereafter insisted they come up. At the end of it all, police took names and addresses, a pleased BBC photographer went away with his scoop, and a disappointed stretcher bearer went off without *his* scoop.

FILMING THE UNLIKELY

A British version of Jim Tyler's Steerman jump (see *Life Jumps Up* p 138), with a balloon substituted for the aircraft, took place over the Sahara in 1980. An additional factor was that Leo Dickinson, adventure cameraman, filmed the sequence, which was described thus:

"When the balloon, piloted by Richard Barr, takes off Dickinson – parachute strapped to his back – is clinging to a nine-metre rope ladder hanging from the bottom of the basket. At 3,600 metres Dave Howerski, a former SAS parachute instructor, jumps from the basket. By releasing hot air the pilot makes the balloon fall faster than Howerski, who is descending in a circling pattern. At 1,200 metres Howerski becomes the first man to parachute from a craft and board it again in mid-air.

'But this leaves two men hanging from the rope ladder – Howerski, who is unable to climb back into the basket because of its overhang, and Dickinson. If they both stay there the balloon will descend too quickly – so Dickinson lets go and parachutes to earth".*

The day before this record-making event, Dickinson, who is no stranger to adventure but was a novice at ballooning, had had an unusually stirring time of it stranded in the Sudanese bush. Choosing to parachute alone from the balloon rather than suffer a bumpy landing with his companions, Dickinson fell out of the sky into the cheetah-charged, lion-lavish bush. Below, crouched over a camp fire, was a tribesman. As he came within conversing distance, Dickinson called – as he thought, reassuringly – "Hello, I'm English!" By way of answer, the terrified tribesman hurled a spear into the air and fled. So did the British balloon, carried by a quickening breeze to a landing point out of sight 13 km away. Dickinson had had his rough landing anyway,

TV Times, December 1980 .

crashing first into a tree and then into a bush, which at least cushioned his legs and prevented any fractures.

His problem was that he didn't know where he was: they'd been drifting in the Sudan but close to the Ugandan border, and for all he knew he might have been in either country. Then he realised that it was only about ten minutes to sunset, after which it would have been utter madness to try to walk anywhere. The full horror of the situation was slow to seep into Dickinson's mind. "I have never been so frightened in my life", he said later. "It came to me how ill-prepared I was. I had five Sudanese pound notes, five boiled sweets, a parachute and a camera. I had no water and already I was absolutely parched. I didn't know what to do".

What he did was to spread the gaily-coloured parachute on the ground, hoping it would be seen from above by his rescuers, and try to light a fire with elephant grass from the embers of the camp fire. Try as he might, however, he couldn't keep the fire burning. When it went out Dickinson climbed into a tree, perched about five metres above the ground, and tried to calm himself. It wasn't easy. For one thing, he couldn't remember whether or not lions climb trees. Had he or had he not seen films of lions dozing on tree branches? . . . And he was thirsty. Within an hour he'd disposed of four boiled sweets and was well on his way to crunching up the last, when prudence restrained him. He took the half-sweet out of his mouth to save for the morning. That idea proved to be half-baked too: "When morning came I couldn't salivate enough to cope with it!" Halfway through the night, Dickinson looked down to see a young lioness circling his parachute. Had he found the circumstances funny, he might have said "Hello, lioness, I'm Leo!" Instead, he just sat there, petrified.

At dawn, Dickinson climbed down from his branch and started walking. Eventually he met a few natives and, with the help of sign language and the five Sudanese pounds, prevailed upon them to guide him to the nearest road, where he was discovered by the balloonists' truck.

"I have never grown up", says Dickinson. "I am a perpetually immature Boy Scout looking for adventure". He insists, though, that all the risks he takes are carefully calculated. Including parachuting impromptu alone, without supplies, into the darkening African bush . . . ? Well, that must be the exception that proves the rule.

THE CURATE'S EGG
— 'something of which parts are excellent' (Chambers Dictionary)

Fresh bread has its attractions for most of us. But who would cycle 112-km across bush country to town and back just to fetch some? The Rev. Geoffrey Howard, that's who.

At the time the curate from Manchester was working in a Nigerian settlement. Several years later, his nutritional preoccupations switched to chocolate cake and strawberry jam. Not surprising, perhaps, when you consider he was crossing the Sahara on foot, from Béni-Abbès in Algeria to Kano in northern Nigeria, pushing 130 kg of food, water and medical supplies in front of him on an oversized Chinese wheelbarrow fitted with a sail.

What, you may ask, is a Chinese wheelbarrow? It's a vehicle with an enormous wheel, some 1.2m in diameter, based on an ancient Chinese design that enabled farmers to push loads many times their own weight. Very suitable, if Howard's success is anything to go by, for crossing 3,200km of desert in a 100-day trek.

Thin, long-haired and bespectacled Geoffrey Howard, then aged 29, was curate of St. Luke's, Manchester, at the time of this odyssey and his motives were both 'incredibly selfish', as he said, and creditably unselfish, as the £1,000 or so he raised for charity through sponsor-ship proved. He also acted as a guinea-pig for the purposes of medical research, which involved, among other things, recording his temperature once every waking hour.

Besides which, this was, in the time-worn phrase, 'something that had never been done before'.

Not one to do something on the spur of the moment – unless it be buying fresh bread – Howard spent 18 months preparing for his effort. His training programme included sleeping in numerous layers of warm clothing and with an electric blanket, running between 14 and 24km a day, dressed to kill in woolly vests, and pushing his wheelbarrow back and forth across the Lancashire moors, clad in the swirling white Arab-style robes he would wear on the trek proper. The sartorial picture was completed by running shoes and a sunhat with a 'chimney' in it, resembling nothing so much as a beehive with a brim.

He set off at Christmas 1974. During the crossing he was backed up by a British Army team of two men in a Land-Rover who replenished his supplies of fresh food and water at prearranged points along the route.

Do curates give in to temptation? Not when the alternative is fatal. "The worst moment was when I had just covered 50km of soft sand", he said. "I came over the top of a ridge and saw the most awful sand dune stretching for 200 metres. If I could have given up or cheated by taking a lift I would have done so. But there was nobody around. It was just a case of going on or lying down to die". At the end of that stretch – the longest, at 405km between waterholes – he was running very low on water and the temperature was around 38C. "I knew that just ahead was a small mining com-munity and that I had to make it to that. I expected it to be a hill-billy collection of shacks, but when I got there it was a fantastic place. The miners, 350 of them and all

69

Europeans, came out to meet me with champagne. I went in to stereo music and upholstered furniture. It was like a dream world, a fantastic oasis, but it was real. Who says there's not someone up there looking after you?"

Someone up there obviously looked after him rather well, seeing him through to the finish-line without serious mishap. There to meet him were his wife and children, Susie, 3, and Sam, 1. He'd missed them even more than the chocolate gateau.

WILD WEST FJORD

Bodø lies on the northern Norwegian coast, above the Arctic Circle, at 67°17'N. There, on the edge of the European continent, it is washed by the Norwegian Sea. Go due west from Bodø and the first land you encounter will be southeast Greenland. Strung out slightly to the north of Bodø are the Lofoten Islands, separated from the Norwegian mainland by the Vestfjorden, a large and hostile stretch of water best known for its substantial fish yield.

In 1954 the first Hawker Hunter jet squadron was established in Bodø. Pilots of Thunderjets contemplated the cruel seas of the region and wondered how they would fare if they had to bail out by parachute into the Vestfjorden with only a dinghy.

22-year-old Knut Hoff, a journalist who today still lives and works in Bodø, together with his friend Knut Jensvoll, a Bodø fireman, offered to find out. The pilots provided them with a dinghy which they inappropriately christened *Bombard* after the famous French sailor-doctor, and they sailed trustingly out of Bodø harbour. It wasn't long before they discovered they'd been palmed off with an old dinghy made in Berlin in 1938. To prove its ancient provenance, the boat was cracked and leaking.

Almost as fast as its sailors pumped air into the supposedly sealed compartments, so it seeped out again. This augured ill, but there was worse to come.

One night the two Knuts slept in a small tent on a tiny island. Somehow they forgot about the incoming tide and when Hoff crawled out of the tent in the morning he found himself up to the wrists in salt water. The island had all but disappeared during the night. They made tea on a Swedish primus stove balanced on the dinghy's soft floor, but the wind and the motion gave them scalding hot mugs of a kind they hadn't wanted. They used the tent as a sail and took turns steering with a long oar lodged in the stern of the boat. While one piloted the boat in its mad flight over the tops of the waves, the other huddled in a sleeping bag.

By the time a few hours had passed they both felt pretty bad – their green faces demonstrated. Early on the morning of the second day, Jensvoll heard a blast of air that he assumed came from a whale. He woke Hoff, who jumped out of his sleeping bag in double-quick time. Fishermen had told him that whales at that time of year (August) are very amorous and will even try to make advances to fishing boats, and Hoff wasn't too keen to mate with a whale. Twice they heard the blast of air – but only when the boat was on top of a big wave. Suddenly they understood why. This was no whale, but the sound of air being squeezed out of the dinghy's airhole. If they couldn't close it, they'd soon be swimming. They became very active very fast.

The way things were going, it wasn't much of a surprise to them that this should happen at the most inopportune moment. They were sailing in the dark. They could make out their destination, the island of Vaeröy, subject of the sinister writings of Edgar Allan Poe and Jules Verne. Between Vaeröy and the southern Lofoten islands is the Moskenes-straumen, a whirlpool with currents more terrifying than almost anywhere else in the world.

Thus far they had struggled for nearly three days and nights against time and the currents. As if this weren't enough, the nearer they got to Vaeröy, the fiercer the contrary seas became. For the last six or seven hours they were paddling for their lives.

Suddenly, as though it had become bored with playing with them, the current just dropped them and then gave them an almighty push, sending them straight up onto dry land as though they'd been driven by an engine. They had travelled ninety km in a dinghy measuring 2.3 x 1.6 metres.

Very tired, they fastened the dinghy to a big stone with a rope and lay down with their faces in the sand. At length, Knut Jensvoll muttered: "Let's get the emergency provisions". His companion got up and trotted over to the boat, where he found six bottles of export beer in the bottom. They emptied them all at once, sitting on the sand with the seagulls crying over their heads, and watching the wind become increasingly stormy and the waves ever more monstrous. If they had still been out there, they mused, they would never have survived.

A few days later the first jet pilot had to bail out over the Vestfjorden and try the experiment himself, for real. He drifted in his dinghy towards Vaeröy – but a helicopter picked him up before he got very far. Alright for some . . .

Stunted Stunt

During World War II, a military pilot, seeing both doors of an airship hangar wide open, flew his machine in one door and out the other – right through the building. And another pilot resolved to earn some prestige points for himself by doing the same.

He waited for his opportunity. One day he saw that the hangar door was open at one end and that mechanics were opening the door at the other end. What he didn't know, and couldn't see from the air, was that this door was just being opened momentarily to allow an aeroplane to be taken out of storage. The daredevil pilot circled, got into a dive, flying very low, and approached the hangar. Now at last he saw, to his horror, that the door at the far end was closed. Too late to change to direction, he swooped into the hangar, throwing his aircraft against all the stored machines to absorb the shock. The impact crushed most of them against the fire doors and wrecked quite a few. The pilot climbed out unhurt.

This little incident did nothing to enhance his prestige.

STRANGER THAN FICTION

'Curiouser and curiouser' cried Alice.
      − Lewis Carroll, *Alice in Wonderland.*

ESCAPE INTO ESCAPISM

Felice Benuzzi was born in Vienna in 1910, of an Italian father and an Austrian mother. As a child he was brought to Trieste and very soon started mountaineering in the Julian Alps and the Dolomites. A trained lawyer, he entered the Colonial Service in 1938, and was appointed a colonial official in Addis Ababa. Then came the war. He was evacuated from Abyssinia (now Ethiopia) with the Italian population after the Allied conquest in 1941, declared a Prisoner of War and taken to Kenya.

354 PoW camp was situated in Nanyuki, at the foot of Mount Kenya. The nearest neutral territory was Portuguese East Africa, a long way away. To reach it one would have needed money, transport, local knowledge, an acquaintance with the main languages and faked documents; and to get home from there presented even greater difficulties. The camp was standard, as prison camps go, a place of boundless frustration, unending emptiness and bland monotony. Benuzzi suffered along with the rest. But just occasionally, fleetingly, as if in a dream, Mount Kenya (5,340 m) peeped out of the clouds, floating on the near horizon. It was the first 5,000-metre peak he had ever seen, and he fell in love with it. It also gave him an idea.

If, he reasoned, there was no means of escaping for good, then at least he would "stage a break in this awful travesty of life". He would try to get out, climb Mount Kenya and return to the camp.

This was not without problems for a prisoner of entirely dependent means. Benuzzi needed companions, equipment, maps and information, food, clothing and time. Not to mention secrecy. Furtive enquiries and carefully directed but veiled discussions eventually led Benuzzi first to one and then to the other of the two men who were to accompany him. He gave up smoking but continued to draw his ration of cigarettes which he exchanged for extra food. He and his companions exercised, collected stores piecemeal, avoided being seen together and met for discussions only at night.

They also read whatever strictly limited sources they could lay hands on – Father F. Cagnolo's work *The Akikuyu* and the *East Africa Annual* for 1942–43 proved useful. So did some tins of 'Kenylon' brand preserved meat and vegetables which arrived in the camp bearing gummed labels that depicted Mount Kenya as seen from the south or south-southwest. But they still had no idea of the configuration of the mountain – not even the number and shape of its peaks. Of the reconnaissance expeditions to Mt. Kenya and ascents by the naturalist Joseph Thomson, by the geologist J.W. Gregory, by Sir Halford Mackinder and by Eric Shipton and P. Wyn Harris who eventually solved many of the problems of Kenya's highest peak Batian in 1929 – of all these Benuzzi and company were at the time monumentally ignorant. To cap it all, newspapers told as did other prisoners, horror stories of buffalo and rhinoceros which roamed the forests on the outskirts of the camp.

Nevertheless, the planning went ahead. What else was there to do?

Benuzzi casually bought, borrowed and stole tools and implements. Much of their equipment, including makeshift crampons, still had to be made, under cover, from scrap – steel from the mudguards and running-boards of cars on a rubbish heap outside the camp (which they visited during work and exercise sorties). From Kenya's highest peak, Batian, in 1929 – of all these Benuzzi and company were monumentally ignorant. To cap it all, newspapers told, as did other prisoners, horror stories of buffalo and rhinoceros which roamed the forests on the outskirts of the camp.

Nevertheless, the planning went ahead. What else was there to do?

Benuzzi casually bought, borrowed and stole tools and implements. Much of their equipment, including makeshift crampons, still had to be made, under cover, from scrap – steel from the mudguards and running-boards of cars on a rubbish heap outside the camp which they visited during work and exercise sorties. From imprints on tar of the compound keys, carelessly left lying on a table by the British Compound Officer, a friendly mechanic cut a duplicate. A tent, complete with pegs and ropes, was acquired by exchange. A thin rope was created by unfastening *fifty* tight knots in a bed-net, and sisal rope collected of the kind issued in the camp for fastening bed-nets onto the bed-frames. A borrowed aluminium water bottle wore a jacket made from blanket remnants. Alcohol from the camp hospital was to be used in a boiler which in turn had been built from empty jam tins. From the pages of an exercise book Benuzzi cut out seventy arrows, to serve as route indicators and painted them red with borrowed enamel. Spread out on his bunk to dry, these had often aroused curiosity amongst fellow prisoners. "Put out more flags", Benuzzi would say cryptically, when questioned, and away they would go, shaking their heads in pity and deeply concerned for his mental welfare. Food was saved, bought, exchanged.

A dress rehearsal for erecting the tent was performed behind the latrines after midnight. The pitch darkness added to the excitement. The break-out had to be particularly carefully planned. And when they made their excape – one Sunday when there was no scheduled afternoon roll call – they left behind a written 'parole' promising to return after the climb.

The climb itself was fraught with every difficulty. Plenty of alarms occurred in the form of human and animal presence – a sawmill, a bull-elephant, tracks, screams, voices. One of the three escapees suffered a fever. The two who had experience of climbing had had no practice for eight years and all had been prisoners of war for the previous two. During the climb itself they were crushed beneath the weight of their rucksacks, deprived of adequate food and forever short of sleep. The attempt was being made in winter; accomplished mountaineers had considered an ascent by this route hopeless even in summer. As if all that were not enough, they had to start their actual attempt on the summit from a base camp which was too low and too far away from the peak. Reluctantly, they abandoned the notion of climbing Batian: their condition and the circumstances forbade an attempt. But the second peak, Lenana, yielded to their 'weak efforts'. Cheerful, they celebrated their achievement by skipping dinner – not that they had much choice.

The return journey was a torture of exhausted, injured bodies and empty stomachs. Eighteen days after their escape, they broke back into the camp, entering the main gate with a working party. Their rucksacks, climbing suits, boots and ice-axes followed them the same day concealed in a lorry among bags of turnips and cabbage. The following morning, they put on clean, freshly ironed clothes and reported to the British Compound Officer. (Before they broke out they had left him a note saying they'd be back in a fortnight.) They were questioned, meticulously searched and confined to cells, though for a somewhat reduced term in recognition of their 'sporting effort'. Rarely have prisoners locked in cells accepted their punishment with such blissful exhilaration, relief and satisfaction.

'Stolen Waters are Sweet' – Proverbs, ix.17
In 1936, Dod Orsborne and three crew sailed from Grimsby to Spain, on via the Canary Islands to Dakar, Senegal, and then via Devil's Island to Georgetown, Guyana (then British Guiana). There he was arrested, sent back to England and tried. Not for sailing the Atlantic, of course, but because the yacht he used, M.F.V. *Girl Pat*, 17.7 metres in length, was stolen.

Departing in a bit of a hurry, Orsborne and crew had a sixpenny coloured school atlas and a ship's compass as their sole navigational aids. On reaching Dakar, they realised that they would have to put to sea again pretty smartly before their limited provisions ran out. As it was, they barely survived the Atlantic crossing and for the last ten days existed entirely without food.

Orsborne made some money from selling his story to a news-ravenous world press and from publishing a book. His earnings doubtless gave him some comfort during the eighteen months' hard labour to which the judge had sentenced him.

VEHICLE VESSELS

A 32-year-old Dutchman, Piet Vroegop, left Norfolk in July 1981 in an attempt to cross the North sea in a Citroën 2CV car with the front wheels replaced by paddles.

Only the North Sea?

In September 1978, Italian explorer Giorgio Amoretti set out from Las Palmas, in the Canary Islands, in an attempt to cross the Atlantic – by Volkswagen.

Amoretti, 46, had been planning the trip for ten years but had virtually no experience as a sailor and even less as a navigator. The 'vessel' consisted of an ordinary Volkswagen Beetle car body, stripped of seats and engine but with its wheels still attached. The inside of the car was filled almost to the roof with expanded polyurethane, which floats so well that it was theoretically 'utterly impossible' for the vehicle to capsize or sink. Amoretti sat on the roof most of the time, reaching down through a hole to reach his provisions. In bad weather, he could take refuge inside – in amongst all the polyurethane.

He carried no radio since he felt this would be an 'inolerable' intrusion into the privacy of his relationship with the sea.

Steering was by means of the front wheels. Oh yes – and because the back of the car was more 'prow'-shaped, he travelled backwards.

Amoretti, you may like to know, went round the world on a Lambretta scooter when he was eighteen, and has crossed the Sahara and parts of Alaska strapped to a kite. Whether this latest venture succeeded or not is anyone's guess, since no-one seems to know what happened or indeed where Amoretti now is.

FAILURE OF BELIEF

"Have we conquered an enemy? None but ourselves", said George Leigh Mallory, who with his inexperienced partner Andrew Irvine disappeared on Mt. Everest at about 8,300 metres on 8th June 1924.

Mt. Everest, which Mallory called 'an infernal mountain, cold and treacherous', is still nobody's friend, though its summit has now borne the tread of over eighty pairs of feet. Prewar, however, the world's highest mountain (8,848 metres) hung, aloof and intractable, a silent challenge, over the heads of aspiring climbers everywhere. And, in one case, of an aspiring non-climber too.

One day in 1932, while sitting in a cafe in Freidburg, Germany, Yorkshireman Maurice Wilson read of the deaths of Mallory and Irvine. The idea came to him that he must try to climb Everest himself, alone: it was the solution to a problem he had harboured for some time. Not long before he had been ill with coughing spasms, presumably tuberculosis, and had seemed certain to die, until a faith healer told him to fast for thirty-five days, taking only sips of water, until his body was purged and he was near death. Then he should ask God to make him well again. Wilson followed the advice and within two months was cured. The power of faith which he had so miraculously experienced was something he wished to share with, and demonstrate to, the world. He cast around for a means to this end but could not find it. Until, at last, there was Everest.

Wilson bought himself a Gipsy Moth, which he named *Ever Wrest*, learned to fly and fought tooth and nail against a strongly opposed British government for permission to fly to Everest. When a telegram from the Air Ministry forbidding the flight came to hand a few minutes before Wilson was due to take off, he simply tore it up and proceeded. He never taught himself to climb, however. For one thing, he had a bad left arm, wounded by machine-gun fire in World War I. For another, there were at that time few ways in which one could learn the techniques and skills of mountaineering other than going out and practising on one's own. Overriding the practicalities was his belief that he had only to fast and pray to establish the direct contact between body and soul which would enable him to reach the summit.

At first Wilson planned to fly as high as possible up the mountain and make a crash landing on the East

Rongbuk Glacier, so that there would be less distance for him to cover on foot. He set off in May 1933 and, by a circuitous route strewn with bureaucratic difficulties, arrived in Lalbalu, India – where the authorities refused him permission to fly over Nepal and impounded his plane to make the point. With this part of the scheme thus foiled, Wilson had to make other plans. Months went by, the monsoon came and went and the attempt on the mountain was postponed until the following year. He managed to sell the plane, which raised some much-needed funds, and made his way to Darjeeling. There he was refused official permission to enter Sikkim and Tibet on foot, so resorted instead to illegal measures. He found three porters who would lead him through Tibet to Base Camp and on 31st March 1934 set out with them, passing rapidly over the border and into the bleak uplands of Tibet. On 14th April, having covered 480 km, he reached Rongbuk monastery and two days later set off alone for Everest, carrying a 20-kg rucksack. Whatever the bulk of the weight consisted of, it did not include many useful items of food or of climbing equipment, such as crampons.

Wholly ignorant of climbing needs and techniques, frustrated by the appalling difficulties of the route, and weakened by glacier lassitude, altitude, snow blindness, pain from his arm wound and the total inadequacy of his 'rations' (a little gruel and a few figs), he was forced to admit temporary defeat. After a nine-day struggle he stumbled back to the monastery where, tended by the Sherpas, he slept for thirty-eight hours and recuperated for a further sixteen days.

On his second attempt he took with him two of the Sherpas, who guided him easily up the East Rongbuk Glacier. At an old camp they found a food dump left over from an earlier expedition. Here he abandoned his near-fast. "All Wilson's dietary plans were cast aside in the face of such bounty. He tucked in willingly to Fortnum and Mason's best foods and finished off with a

1-lb. [450 gm] box of 'King George' chocolates".* Leaving
the Sherpas in the camp, Wilson struck out again for the
North Col. He was away for four days, making creeping,
arduous progress on extremely exposed terrain until,
about six hundred metres below the summit, he came to
a twelve-metre ice wall split by a chimney – a barrier
that had summoned up the best efforts of so skilled a
climber as Frank Smythe in 1933. Hour after hour he
tried to climb the chimney, and failed. Exhausted, and
without food and water, he returned to the camp and
rested for two days. The Sherpas tried to persuade him
to return to Rongbuk, but Wilson could not be swayed.
His last attempt began on 31st May. It is reasonable to
suppose that the ice chimney again stood between him
and a final ascent, while his own pride and stubbornness
stood between him and a final descent. He died, presumably of exhaustion and exposure, asleep in his tent.

Wilson's corpse was found the following year by Eric
Shipton's expedition. Charles Warren described the
circumstances, noting three peculiar facts: "(1) No sleeping bag was to be found. (2) He was within 200 yards of
the 1933 Everest expedition's food dump, which he knew
about because he had already made use of it. (3) He was
within hailing distance of Camp 3 where Tewang [one
of the Sherpas] was supposed to have been waiting for
him".**

Beside him lay his diary of the expedition and – bizarre
addition to an already singular story – some women's
clothing and a book in which the hapless 'ascetic' had
recorded extravagant sexual fantasies ...

He was buried in a crevasse and a cairn was built at
the spot where the body had lain. In 1960 the story took
another macabre turn when a Chinese expedition redis-

*Walt Unsworth: *Everest*. London, Allen Lane, 1981. p.
243.
**Charles Warren's diary.

covered Wilson's body, which had emerged from the glacier with the movement of the ice, and again buried the strange Englishman on the mountain of his savaged dreams.

Exile in a Cage
Jaromir 'Watch this Space' Wagner, who in 1980 flew the Atlantic strapped to the pylon of a light aircraft, and in 1981 set up a speed roller-skating record in Hockenheim, has other ideas up his Czech sleeve. The latest, which he acknowledges to be the most dangerous to date, is to cross the Atlantic in a cage.

The plan, announced in July 1982, was for a Polish container ship to tow the steel cage, six metres long and three metres high, from Hamburg to New York, via Rotterdam. Nothing but a few empty fifty-litre barrels would hold the cage out of the water, so that Wagner would be exposed, day and night, to temperatures of 14C at most. To combat the cold, the 43-year-old adventurer planned to wear a wetsuit of the kind developed for use by divers on oilrigs.

Whether he proposed to cook fish on a Primus or live off scraps of *kasha* thrown to him by the sailors is not reported.

THE HEADMAN WHO COULD PANDA TO AMERICAN TASTES

Nowadays the panda, symbol of the World Wildlife Fund and darling of zoo visitors throughout the world, is a familiar beast, its success or failure in the business of reproduction a frequent topic for the press.

Fifty or so years ago, however, few Westerners had ever seen a panda. So, some time in the late 1920s, Gerald Russell, an eccentric American, heir to the fortune of the Morgan family of New York, went to Burma to try to find and capture and bring back a couple of pandas. Accompanying him was a girl called Ruth Harkness.

They were vastly and generously equipped, amply funded and fondly supported by the American zoological societies. They sailed to Mandalay and trekked up-country to the edge of the mountain forests. There they decided to dump their animal cages and most of their heavy equipment, so as to make a faster-moving sortie. They left their equipment with the headman of a high hill village and set off on foot with a bunch of Burmese porters.

They searched the northeastern hill areas of Burma and a couple of times even crossed the invisible border in that wild country that took them into China. They covered hundreds of km of forest, negotiated hundreds of muscle-cracking hills, struggled with the rain, the wet, the leeches and the cold, put up with miserable food, argued with rebellious porters. For six arduous months they did this; and not a panda anywhere. No sight, no sound, no whiff of panda.

They returned to the edge of the plains and to the hill village from which they had set out. Their heavy equipment was intact and in good order: the headman had done his job well and was able to hand everything over just as they had left it. But he was curious.

What had they been doing up there in that wild hill country all this time? Had they been looking for something, and if so what?

They had been looking for a *dzhu*, they told him; the Burmese Panda, as it was known there; a Chinese Panda, the Chinese called it.

"The dzhu?" he said. "You mean that you were looking for a dzhu all this time? To capture? To take home with you?"

And he led them round to the back of his grass hut where, in a little compound with bamboo walls, was a fully grown, perfectly healthy, perfectly genuine dzhu.

"Why," said the headman, "if you had asked me when you were here six months ago I would have sold you *my* dzhu!"

Gerald Russell and Ruth Harkness paid the good headman six dollars for the animal and took it home with them.

And so the first panda was introduced to the Western world.

Plenty More Fish in the Sea

In 1978 Don Cameron and crew almost flew across the Atlantic in a balloon. There had been fifteen previous attempts. As it happened, the next one, very shortly after Cameron's, was successful.

While waiting to make the flight from St. John's, Newfoundland, Cameron and his party sat in the restaurant of a local hotel trying to decide what they should order for dinner. Cameron, a sometimes-dour Scot, commented to the assembly: "We'll all eat fish. The more we eat of them, the less of them there are to eat us".

When Cameron's balloon landed in the Bay of Biscay, only 160 km from the French coast and success, it was in the middle of a fishing fleet and ironically he was rescued by a trawler.

ABOMINABLE SANDMAN

History tells us (or tells those of us interested in the remote and the esoteric) that a great city called Ubar once existed in a then fertile oasis on the southern edge of the Empty Quarter of Arabia. Described as the 'Atlantis of the Sands', Ubar is said to have been a large marbled city, dominated by a great red fortress encrusted with rubies and silver. It was renowned not only for its wealth but also for the wickedness of its inhabitants, the Ad tribe, who were punished for their sins by being turned into *Nisnas*, one-eyed, one-armed half-monkeys. Ubar then fell into ruin, as any city would, its once famous gardens known as the *Jannat ad* ('the Paradise of Ad') withered and died, and the city was swallowed up by the sands.

Or perhaps not. In December 1930, while crossing the Wadi Mitan in the area where the Oman-Saudi Arabia border now runs, the British explorer Bertram Thomas came across "well worn tracks about a hundred yards in cross section, graven in the plain". One of his Rashidi camel-men explained that these tracks led across the sands to the city of Ubar. What is more, the cameleer recalled as a boy having seen "two large white rounded blocks of stone, notched at the edge both alike, but each so big as to require two men to lift it". He was able to give the location of these stones, which he clearly believed to be the remains of the city.

To go back to the *Nisnas* for a moment. According to the *Geographical Dictionary* of Yaqut (1179–1229), an Arab traveller staying with the Mahri people raised the subject of the *Nisnas* and was told by his host: "We hunt it and eat it, and it is a beast with one arm and one leg, and it has no other members". When the Arab asked to see one, a *Nisnas* was captured the following day and brought to him. He described the creature as having 'a face like a man except it was only half a face', with one arm attached to the chest, and with one leg. The *Nisnas* spoke to the Arab, saying "By God and by you", which the listener apparently took as a plea for mercy. He urged that the *Nisnas* be released. His host, however, told him not to be deceived by the creature's words, for "it is our food". Eventually it was released and ran swiftly away.

History, being itself a capricious beast, does not relate how a creature with one leg was able to run. Nevertheless, the Koran also reports that the *Nisnas* were formerly men who were transformed into beasts by an early prophet as a punishment.

In archaeological terms the *Nisnas* are a bit of a side issue (rather like that arm issuing from the chest . . .). But they do add a pinch of spice to the story of the lost city – of which, incidentally, nothing has been seen since Bertram Thomas' day, despite the mounting of several expeditions to search for it.

Why am I telling you this anyway?

Because Major Charles Weston-Baker, a member of the Sultan of Oman's Armoured Regiment, is in his spare time trying to find Ubar, using the technique of aerial survey. He operates from a hot-air balloon called *Sky Chariot*, escorted on the ground by an armoured car squadron or desert Land-Rovers. So far, he has found Neolithic sites, mounds, bones and hewn (but not dressed) stones and has been shown places where wells yield limitless supplies of fresh water – but no Ubar. Weston-Baker is coordinating the Oman phase of Operation Raleigh and, by the time its keen young explorers arrive on the scene in 1987–8, he hopes to have access to an American satellite which can detect water underground. Where there is good water, so there may be the site of an ancient city.

As scientific ventures go, this one offers better than average opportunities for the spectator. So if a leg-hopping *Nisnas has* happened to linger on in those parts and encounters balloon-hopping modern man, it will doubtless stop in its single track, clutch its hand to its half-head in amazement, and watch with its eye popping out.

Archer Hits the Target

As everybody knows, it is illegal to collect sea-ears on Guernsey except during the first four days after the full moon. Sea-ears are a type of mollusc, rightly prized as a delicacy and protected by an age-old statute on the island.

Enter left from the water wings, one day in 1969, David Kempthorne Ley, behaving for all the world as if he were not acquainted with the law, to begin prising the shellfish off a rock with a hook – out of season. Acting on a tip-off, Police-Sergeant David Archer from St. Peter Port set off in a wetsuit and pursuit. He swam along the seabed in seventeen metres of water, approached the offender from behind and tapped him on he shoulder. When they got to the surface, the Sergeant revealed his identity. Back at the police station, Ley was fined £20 and had his diving equipment confiscated. Archer may not have known it at the time, but he had just made the world's first underwater arrest.

HUGE MONSTER NOT SEEN IN HIMALAYAS

Around about the late 1940s, two British scientists called J.P. Mills, MA, CSI, CIE, and C.R.S. Stonor, BSc (a former Assistant Curator of the London Zoo under Julian Huxley), with the backing of some learned societies went on an expedition to Assam to a region marked on maps with a blank – unexplored. There they discovered a tribe known as the Apa Thanis who lived in a fertile valley in the mountains. Mills and Stonor were shown burial mounds of four reptiles, about as big as crocodiles, which the ancestors of the Apa Thanis had exterminated by burying them alive. The natives, like most illiterates, had a very vivid tribal memory and were able to give what appeared to be an accurate description of the creatures, which had been handed down from father to son. The animals were like nothing known to science. It was said that in another valley, eight km distant, the creatures could be seen in a swamp which became a lake when it filled with water at the height of the summer monsoon.

Assam is the wettest place in the world and conditions in the forest in the rainy season are appalling. On the trip to the Apa Thanis' valley, Mills' daughter was stricken with malaria and died almost overnight. After their return to Britain, Stonor remained fascinated by the story he had heard of the second – further – valley. He determined to mount an expedition to visit it. Ralph Izzard, a British journalist and explorer, persuaded his employers, *The Daily Mail*, to put up the money. Sir Akbar Hydari, then Governor of Assam, became the expedition's sponsor, at the urging of the British 'Establishment' in India, and Lord Mountbatten, then Viceroy, became patron. Mills and Stonor had meanwhile published a paper on their subject entitled *A traditional account of the survival within historic times of a large aquatic reptile in the outer Himalayas of Assam*.

The hunt was on.

However, no-one, in particular no scientist, wanted to lose face if the reptile failed to come to light, and the new expedition was sworn to deadly secrecy. If they found nothing, they agreed that the whole episode would be quietly forgotten and not a word published about it.

The trek to the 'lost valley' of Rilo in 1948 was

thoroughly dreadful, made worse by the fact that Izzard suffered a broken collar-bone. Once there, they built a blind and sat up in it, watching the lake for the Buru (as the creature was known) and waited. And waited. For weeks. And saw nothing.

The valley of Rilo was entirely surrounded by cliffs and mountains and had no cleft through which water could escape. When the party arrived, the entire floor, except for a patch of clear water in the centre about as big as four tennis courts, was covered by a mass of thick green weeds. According to local tribesmen, when the monsoon reached its height the waters spread and became a vast lake. Sure enough, the rains pelted down for a few weeks and the level of the water rose. But so too, rising on top of the water, did the weeds. It became something of an obsession among the British observers to try to reach the clear patch, but for a long time they could think of no way of doing so. At length, they constructed two bamboo ladders and began to leapfrog one over the other across the weeds. This proved distressingly difficult work and after they had covered nearly a kilometre they abandoned the attempt and in desperation set off, ladderless, across the quaking weeds which barely took their weight. They reached the pool but on the edge of it the weeds gave way and in went Izzard up to his neck.

Just as he was casting about for a way to get out, a huge eruption occurred in the water beside him and Izzard was catapulted like a jack-in-the-box onto a firm patch of weed before he had time to think. Fully convinced that a monster had indeed appeared and was about to drag him down by the heels, Izzard looked about, shaken. Nothing.

What had in all probability happened was that he had released a great bubble of marsh gas. It was almost impossible to gauge the depth of the water in that repulsive and hostile place but our explorers guessed from the inclination of the surrounding slopes that the bottom could have been a hundred metres or more down, though how much was mud and how much water they never found out. Izzard had probably, in those few instants, been well out of his depth.

Abandoning the search for the Buru, the party made their way back to civilisation, the trek out being reportedly even worse than the trek in. Arriving empty-handed, they found Assam and a good deal of India in uproar. Somewhere in the chain of command there had been a leak and the story had reached the Indian press. As no-one could tell them exactly what the expedition was after, they invented their own animals, and a very good job they made of them too.

Headline: EXTINCT MAMMAL'S STRIDE ALONG HIMALAYAN BORDER. The text, in *The Hindusthan Standard* of 5th May 1948, began:

"A Dinotherium, a member of a race of huge, prehistoric mammals, till now believed to be totally extinct, has been seen perambulating in the southern side of the Himalayan Range bordering on Assam . . . Tribal people of the frontier tract of Balipara recently came across this moving mountain of flesh wandering majestically and happily plucking the tops of huge ancient trees . . ."

Carried away on the tide of his own imagination, the writer took it away from there.

Izzard and party were besieged by journalists wanting confirmation and details of their sightings. How many monsters had they seen? None. Well then, how big were they? There were none. But how dangerous were they? There were no monsters. Why were the explorers so reticent? They had seen nothing.

But the newspapers had given accounts of the sightings and a description of the monster. There it was, in black and white.

So why – oh, terrifying thought – why were the explorers holding out on them?

Five Minus One Equals Five

One day in Northumbria a Coastguard saw a group of five canoeists returning from the Farne Islands. He noted that one was having trouble balancing his kayak. Sure enough, the canoeist very soon after tipped out into the sea and at the same time his kayak disappeared from view. The Coastguard, who knew an emergency when he thought he saw one, sprang into action. He alerted the helicopter, informed HQ at Edinburgh and called out the inshore lifeboat from Seahouses, six km down the coast. He then finished his entry in the logbook and idly looked out to sea again.

To his consternation, he now saw *five* canoeists, calmly making very good progress towards the shore. No sign of trouble. No-one missing. No one in the water way back. He counted them, again and again. Always five. Yet he had clearly seen one kayak sink.

What the lookout didn't know was that the five canoeists had developed a 'self-rescue' technique of emptying a kayak in deep water using one or two others as a fulcrum over which to rock it. The whole manoeuvre had been carried out deliberately, allowing that canoeist to continue paddling as before. Meanwhile, the emergency rescue services were determined to carry out an emergency rescue. They pulled the offending kayak on board the lifeboat and managed to break it in two, and dragged the reluctant paddler after it, leaving one of his shoes behind.

BEYOND THE PALE

Is there something curious about the polar regions? Dr. Andrés Solanot of Argenina thinks so. And if he succeeds in mounting his expedition to Antarctica he may be right, because one of the curious things there will then be Dr. Solanot himself.

Maybe one does him an injustice, but as his present scheme stands, it's difficult even to establish what exactly it is he's trying to prove.

Some facts: Dr. Fridtjof Nansen, the Norwegian explorer, noticed in the 1890s that as he sailed towards the North Pole, the climate, unexpectedly, softened above 70–75 degrees latitude and certain large expanses of sea were free of ice.

Admiral Richard Byrd, an American, travelling in the Arctic in the 1920s and again in the 1940s, reported seeing strange phenomena – vegetation, forested mountains and something resembling a large animal – in an area where there ought to have been nothing but an ice desert.

During the U.S.-constituted Operation Highjump expedition to the Antarctic in 1946–47, one Commander Bunger discovered in longitude 104^{0}E the so-called Bunger's Oasis – an area of almost square temporary lakes, non-volcanic, with water warmer than that of the ocean, coloured very blue or sometimes green with pink reflections, containing algae and lower forms of life.

Now some speculation: Dr. Solanot asserts that many polar explorers – including Nansen, Byrd, the Australian G.H. Wilkins, the Russian Dumbrova, and Byrd's colleague Rear-Admiral Dufek – all saw and referred, in mysterious and highly unspecific terms, to lands *beyond the pole* in both Arctic and Antarctic regions. Great new territories were said to exist 'beyond' the poles.

Now even Dr. Solanot knows that if you travel in any direction from the North Pole you are heading south;

from the South Pole, north. Also, that while magnetic and astronomical conditions in the polar regions may make it difficult, it should never be impossible to pinpoint one's exact location. Yet Wilkins, Dufek and Byrd all, according to Solanot, used the words 'beyond the pole', failing abjectly to give their longitude and latitude at the time of their great discovery. Perhaps, conjectures Solanot, astronomical readings indicated that the explorers had reached the South Pole while gyroscopic compasses continued to indicate that their direction of movement was southwards.

Here we enter dreamland. Dr. Solanot wishes to find the great new territories 'beyond the pole' and has delineated an area of the Antarctic which is the most likely to yield what he is looking for (whatever that is). To do so, he intends to reproduce the conditions which prevailed when Byrd surveyed the territory: to set up a land base, to conduct the search in January, to use an aeroplane with skis and above all to fly low and slowly. "Something strange happens in the South Pole", Dr. Solanot pronounces, "and if we want to know what it is about, we shall have to go and watch. Perhaps" he goes on "some of you will be with us in spirit when we fly, looking for the shadow of a shadow, *beyond* the South Pole".

Meanwhile, a modern expert on Antarctica confesses that the entire notion, together with the claims attributed to the polar explorers of history, is Greek to him. "It's the sort of thing" he says "I usually put away in a file labelled *Curiosa*".

Putting on his Sinking Cap
British dottiness has a long history.
Back in July 1899, an Englishman who called himself 'Professor Miller' set off from Atlantic City, New Jersey, to attempt to *walk* to Britain. His 'shoes', one and a half metres long, looked rather like miniature birchbark canoes serrated along the bottom. His 'rescue' boat, captained by William Andrews, was a fold-up gaff cutter, *Doree*, only 3.7 metres long. The plan was for Andrews to accompany the Professor all the way, acting as a kind of mobile cafeteria and boarding house. Unfortunately for the two misguided gentlemen, and for marine historians, the Professor did not get very far before giving up, doubtless with his enthusiasm and his mortar board dampened.

Box of Tricks
In 1956 Warwick Deacock, explorer, adventurer and tour leader, was in Alaska. His then girlfriend, Antonia van den Bos, went into London's exclusive Fortnum's and asked for a gift 'suitable for an officer on a glacier in Alaska'. "Certainly, modom," the assistant replied, "follow me". And he led her to the confectionery department. Deacock received the present in a parcel by way of an air drop. There was no letter or address label, but somehow he knew who the sender was. He returned home and married the girl with the sense of humour that matched his own – the start, she says, of a still continuing joke.
What was in the box? Glacé fruits.

INVENTION AND INTERVENTION

The Knight said ... 'It's my own invention.'
 – Lewis Carroll, *The Walrus and the Carpenter,*
Through the Looking Glass.

LA DONNA E MOBILE

The experience of seaman Ronald E. Johnson suggests that, if you submit to the whims of the elements, of time and of the vessel itself, you can get almost anywhere you want – well, *some*where, anyway – as surely as if you set yourself up in control. It helps if you are aboard a sound hull and have some idea how to behave at sea.

Johnson, then 38, left Honolulu harbour in October 1947 under tow from a sub-chaser, which he hoped would take him all the way to Tahiti. He too was on board a sub-chaser, an unpowered, unconverted, thirty-three-metre vessel with the number *SC671* and no name, the repository of all his savings. The tandem travellers had only been gone a day when heavy weather made light work of two tow lines. The crew of the tug tried to persuade Johnson to give up the idea of the crossing, but without success. Johnson took some provisions on board and decided to try and make Tahiti on his own.

From a roll of canvas and some odd timbers he constructed three squaresails and spars and rigged them up in the least inappropriate places. *SC671* took practically no notice of the man at the helm and insisted on rounding her stern into the wind. Johnson gave the lady her head and sailed along backwards, in the trough of the waves. This worked fine. Occasionally current, wind

Top: Rüdiger Nehberg on his 'survival march' through Germany, carrying the sum total of his equipment and a dead squirrel collected to eat along the way.
Bottom: Nehberg in southern Germany. The final equation: pounds lost, years gained.
Germany's Fruit and Nut Case (Rüdiger Nehberg)

Christian-Yves Nau in Paris in 1973 sailing his landyacht down the Elysian Fields towards triumph.
Sailing Through Paris (Christian-Yves Nau)

Top: David Springbett improving his physique by sprinting between Concorde and helicopter during his bid on the world record for a scheduled trans-Atlantic flight.
Bottom: Lucky David Springbett, a reinsurance broker and 1981's Salesman of the Year, can afford a watch.
Going Round the World Makes the World Go Round (David Springbett)

El Capitan dominates the skies, Legal Officers and rangers rule Yosemite National Park, and Robin Heid dangles in between.
Taking Flight in Yosemite (Robin Heid)

David Hempleman-Adams, who ventured alone onto the Arctic ice in 1983. The North Pole eluded him. Inset: Hempleman-Adams looking for the Pole on his expedition but failing to spot a single pole anywhere.
Try, Try Again **(Stephen Vincent)**

Volker Lenzer and motorcycle on Australia's Nullarbor Plain. The tree is the exception that proves the rule.
I'm Gringo. Fly Me (Volker Lenzner)

Top: The *Sierra Sagrada* ('Holy Mackerel') — half-catamaran, half-box, in which Francis Brenton twice crossed the Atlantic.
Bought a Crooked Cat, Sailed a Crooked Mile (D.H. Clarke)

Bottom: Warwick Deacock and pals displayed a fine cheek during their voyage down the Daly River, Australia, in boats made from packing cases.
Daly of Delight (Warwick Deacock, Ausventure)

Top: The late John Waterman climbing in the Shawangunks, New York State, in about 1968, aged 16.
Bottom: Mt. Hunter, in Alaska. The southeast spur, climbed solo by John Waterman in 1978, is the prominent buttress in the centre of the picture: rock below, snow and ice above.
Fire in the Snow (Guy Waterman)

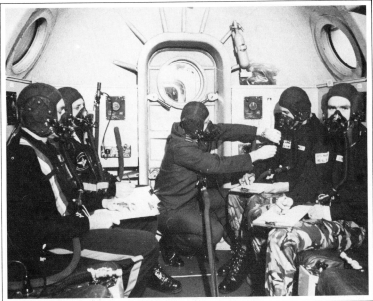

Top: Parachutist at about 3,600 metres over the English Channel. The team needed Courage when they reached France, where the gendarmerie and farmers alike made them feel thoroughly unwelcome.
(Roger Allen)
Bottom: High altitude chamber test for 'Operation Courage' – parachuting across the Channel.
'All Goes if Courage Goes' (Ted Lewington)

Top: Charles Shea-Simonds' Tiger Moth in fine fettle.
Middle: One of the many charms of a Tiger Moth is that it looks much the same upside-down as the right way up. Just after dawn in the Dawn to Dusk Rally 1982.
Bottom: Blushingly, the plane buries its face in the corn. Neither AC nor DC was the right current in the freakishly inauspicious weather conditions that foiled her flight that day.
Tiger in the Corn (Charles Shea-Simonds)

Top: The Skiing Tuareg on the powder sand of the Saharan dunes.
The Skiing Tuareg (Hadji Adberrahmane)

Bottom: Per Arne Jeremiassen operating on a high advertising budget.
No Bridge Too Far (Per Arne Jeremiassen)

Top: Per Arne Jeremiassen competing in a bathtub race in Norway. To make things more interesting, he deliberately pulled the plug on his own entry and ended up sitting for hours on a pole in the fjord. Nobody noticed his absence. Bottom: Norwegians and Finns breaking the rules by parachuting from the Europabrücke in Austria: anyone can see that pedestrians are not permitted on this bridge.

No Bridge Too Far (Per Arne Jeremiassen)

Top: Four hopeful Saharan travellers, from Hendon, London, with their two Land-Rovers, Fred and Charlie.
Bottom: And then there was one. A drastic method of sending smoke signals, as Land-Rover Charlie goes up in flames.
Make Straight in the Desert a Highway . . . (Richard Slowe)

Left: Trekking in Nepal — heavily laden, sometimes sorefooted, but still gay.
Heights of Enjoyment
(Philip Judson)

Right: Batian Peak, Mt Kenya, from the northwest. The upper part of the sunny speck is the pitch where the three POWs were beaten — by exhaustion, illness and the lack of any kind of suitable equipment.
Escape into Escapism
(Sergio Masini)

Aerial survey in the 'Empty Quarter' of the Arabian Peninsula. Charles Weston-Baker, escorted by desert patrol car, looking for the lost city of Ubar — or for the legendary, one-eyed, one-armed, one-legged *Nisnas*.
Abominable Sandman (Charles Weston-Baker)

Top: Did he fall or was he pushed? Hang gliding underwater in Wales.
Underwater Risibility (Fred Walton)

Bottom: Proving the economic forecasters wrong: low inflation in Brazil.
How Brazilian Ballooning Went Like a Bomb (Robert Rechs)

or caprice turned her round to face forwards, in which case Johnson would obligingly shift the masts. Then, when she adopted her usual unladylike stance, with her rear presented forwards, Johnson would simply rerig the canvas and spars. The frequent readjustments caused him a lot of work, but Johnson had energy, resignation and, above all, time on his side.

Together, sailor and vessel sidled crab-like across the seas for four months, drifting in the general direction of the Fiji Islands. After covering in this fashion a distance of some 4,800 km, they met a vessel which towed them the last 500 kms to land. They made Suva on 12th February 1948. This wasn't exactly where Johnson had wanted to go, but at least it wasn't where he'd started from either.

HANGING LOOSE

It is −20C and you are sitting in a snow hole at about 4,250 metres above sea level on top of Les Grandes Jorasses with an Italian-born mountain guide. You have been trapped on the mountain for some twenty hours. Three of your colleagues have been rescued by helicopter but the pilot is unable to come in for you until the solid cloud clears momentarily, which it steadfastly refuses to do.

Not the cosiest of situations. Yet this was the predicament Londoner Rory McCarthy found himself in during April 1981.

Hang-gliding as a sport is, if not in its infancy, then at least in its Action-Man-and-Meccano childhood, an age from which McCarthy, then 20, was not himself far removed. Hang-glider pilots have to fly from some high point and sooner or later someone was bound to want to fly from the summit of Mt. Blanc. A handful of pilots have done it. Then along came McCarthy, aiming to take along for the flight a complete beginner called John Moody, in a tandem machine. For five months beforehand, they did the rounds of sponsors and donors, tugging at heart- and purse-strings and twisting arms until they had the £16,000 it would take to mount the venture. They expected to raise a further £150,000 for charity through personal sponsorship.

From the beginning, the cards were stacked against them. For days the weather was bad, with a lot of cloud and rain, forcing postponement after postponement until a clear – and hot – day dawned. Then Mt. Blanc decided to play Snow Maiden: the helicopter pilot couldn't land his craft on the mountain because of huge snow drifts on the summit. The team swallowed the setbacks and switched to a new target, the neighbouring peak of Les Grandes Jorasses. Then a contrary wind whistled in to stir things up. A two-man jump was no longer feasible. Moody was flown back to base and a substitute plan adopted for McCarthy and his companions Nick Gifford and Howard Edwards to fly solo. Together with the guide, Renato Petigax, and a newspaper photographer, the three flyers and their equipment were flown in relays up to the summit. They assembled the hang-gliders, taking care not to skimp on safety precautions but glancing increasingly nervously at the clouds that came rolling towards them.

Suddenly they were in it. Cloud, cold and minimum visibility were the doom-laden trio of invaders. Nick Gifford, in a valiant but panic-driven bid to score at least one flight for the day, sprinted down the mountain towards take-off but tripped and fell in the soft snow and had to be dragged back from the edge.

A radio call summoned help from the helicopter. But though the pilot hovered nearby waiting to seize the moment to swoop in, it was six hours before he could land. Meanwhile, knowing that the craft could take no more than three passengers at once, the five adventurers set upon each other to argue the toss, for the most part verbally but with a few tears and raised fists thrown in. The argument, curiously enough, was not about who would go in the first lift but about who wanted to stay. Rory McCarthy felt it his duty, as team leader, to stay behind; but so did Howard Edwards, McCarthy's former tutor and mentor. A fleeting break in the cloud and in swooped the helicopter 'like a bat out of hell', removing to safety the reluctant Edwards, Gifford – now weak from lack of oxygen – and the photographer. Two and a half more hours passed. By now it was 8 pm, dark was falling and the pilot had to call off his rescue attempts for the night.

And so it was that McCarthy and Petigax had to dig in their heels and wait. Petigax was for trying to climb down the mountain, but McCarthy, a non-climber, didn't rate his chances of succeeding high enough to want to opt for that measure. Convinced for a time that he was going to die, McCarthy put the farewell machinery in motion: by walkie-talkie he sent messages of condolence for his own death to his parents and girlfriend; he made a tape 'saying goodbye to the world'. At the same time, the instinct for survival and the guide's mental stamina shot holes in the layer of defeatism. They donned all their warm clothing, including helmets (which substantially reduce heat loss from the body), dug a snow hole, wrapped a parachute over their heads, rubbed their legs to maintain circulation and tried to keep each other cheerful.

6.30 am seemed to take forever to arrive, but at last the rescue operation was under way again. In the intense silence, they could hear the chopper blades way below in the town. And as the day dawned the weather cleared long enough for the helicopter to whisk the two survivors off the mountain.

Having survived the experience feeling only slightly ill, McCarthy's team caused quite a bit of ill feeling elsewhere. The Delta (hang-gliding) Club of Chamonix complained that it had not been contacted before the attempt and that the team broke local rules by taking off and landing on ski slopes and flying in marginal meteorological conditions. The British Hang Gliding Association was also irritated by having been kept in the dark, especially since two of the pilots were members of the Association. The Secretary observed: "The affair has received a great deal of bad publicity on television and in the press and the sport has not gained from it. I imagine that those involved feel chastened by their experiences".

Far from it. "It changed me as a person and in some ways for the worse", McCarthy told a reporter. "I find that now I can't tolerate pettiness, I can't tolerate stupid people. Things have to be fast and they have to be precise and I tend to lose my temper far more now... An experience like mine should make you value life a lot more but it had quite the reverse effect on me. I'm crazier than ever now".

And to prove it, McCarthy began to plan two more extraordinary flights.

The current altitude record for a hang-glider stood, in late 1982, at 9,600 metres. The charity for which McCarthy was hoping to raise money this time was the Stoke Mandeville Hospital, where paraplegics, amputees and others with serious physical injuries and disabilities are treated (draw your own conclusions). First he was to do a tandem jump from a balloon at something over 7,000 metres. This was to be a practice flight for a solo attempt on the world record, at Edwards Air Force Base, California – best known as the landing site for the Space Shuttle – using special insulation and oxygen equipment. The projected height for this jump? Nearly 11,000 metres, 2,000 metres higher than Everest.

Banana Split

In the desert the initials A.A. might just as well stand for All Alone, because that's what you are when it comes to emergencies and breakdowns.

Bill Johnson was the fitter in a desert Patrol, travelling from Siwa Oasis towards Benghazi, Syria. They had travelled for several days fairly uneventfully when the truck in front of Johnson's suddenly lurched well over a metre into the air. The driver reckoned he had hit a rock. When Johnson investigated, he found oil pouring from the gearbox which was badly cracked. They drove on for a bit and made camp.

The following morning just as dawn was breaking, Johnson heard a voice and saw a Bedu driving a flock of goats and sheep in the distance. He woke his mate, who spoke good Arabic.

"Go and ask that Arab if he'll give us some bananas in exchange for tea and flour". The little errand was successful.

Johnson removed the top of the gearbox. Then he peeled all the bananas and stuffed it with the skins. Thus repaired, the gearbox served them well, before a replacement was fitted at base, for another 1,400 km. Johnson does not report whether all that banana flesh was added to the desert or their diet.

A RARE GAS

Anthony Smith is co-founder and President of the British Balloon and Airship Club and as such flies balloons a lot. Ballooning is not intrinsically funny – though many people think so, connecting it no doubt with the flying of children's toy balloons. Real full-sized balloons are technically complex vehicles and when things go awry in their handling the outcome is likely to be unfortunate, tragic, or at best merely tedious. But just occasionally ballooning gets funny.

One year, Smith left his balloon in storage in Belgium. Collecting the balloon, Smith forgot to check the ropes – which had rotted. The subsequent flight raised a few hairs and eyebrows, as ropes parted at inconvenient moments. Somehow he and his crew managed to bring the balloon down in a field, but – again owing to rope failure – they were unable, operating from the ground, to deflate it. There the balloon stood, towering defiantly twenty-five metres above them.

There is an alternative method of collapsing a balloon, without using ropes: a valve at the very top. How, though, to reach it? The obvious choice was the fire brigade, yet Smith and company were nervous about the expense they imagined a call would incur. Perhaps before calling the firemen out they should have a fire? How about starting one in the barn nearby? Compensation to the farmer would surely work out cheaper than paying the fire service. In the end, reason – and cowardice – won the day and they called for help.

The fire engines had suitably long ladders, and even a baby ladder angling downwards from the tip. Smith climbed up, then down, and reached the valve. Turning it, he was engulfed and almost overwhelmed by the tremendous gush of gas escaping from the top. The gas which almost swept him away was helium.

Now, helium is not only a rare gas, it also has an exceedingly rare effect on the vocal chords. Swim around in a helium atmosphere and you turn instantly into the aural equivalent of Donald Duck.

So there stood our premier British balloonist, surrounded by billowing swathes of balloon, silently cursing his own inattention to routine rope checks, and *squeaking* to the uncomprehending Flemish-speaking firemen below: "Take it down! Take it down!"

Fortunately the helium-induced fever pitch wears off quickly. Returning to the ground, and to normal, Anthony Smith was able to reassure the worried throng by delivering his 'Thank you' to the firemen in a rock-bottom bass voice.

Mad Englishman Out in the Midday Sun

Since snowshoes cannot readily be bought in Britain, the committed explorer may have to resort to making his own. Doing just that one beautiful July day was a student, destined to join an expedition to Greenland. As he sat on the edge of the M6 waiting for his arranged lift to Glasgow airport, he was hurriedly making snowshoes from polythene tubing and thin bamboo. A boy came up and watched the student threading twine. "What are you making?" asked the observer. "Snowshoes", replied the man carelessly. The boy stiffened and tiptoed away. Shortly afterwards an ambulance drew up to remove the waiting explorer. It seemed a man had gone missing from a mental home . . .

Self-Supporting Salesman

In August 1964, an American ice-cream salesman by the name of Leo Ledoux set out to cross the Atlantic without even a plank for support. Launching himself from Miami Beach, he floated restfully on his back for 32 hours and 38 minutes. By this time he was still rather a long way from the other side, having covered only 130 km before giving up the attempt.

ARTICLES OF FAITH

Like that other notable carpenter of nearly 2,000 years before, Ira C. Sparks, from Peru, Indiana, didn't just saw wood: he saw visions of a better world. His duty, as he perceived it, was to pass on the Gospel to the spiritually ignorant, which meant taking The Word to India and the Holy Land.

Also, like his predecessor, a man of modest means, Sparks had to use the humblest mode of transport. He built a comfortable packing crate, stocked it with food and water, labelled it 'personal effects' (value $US 15) and had it shipped to himself, at a cost of $24.42, from San Francisco to Bombay via Hong Kong. When loaded onto the *Taiyo Maru*, of the Toyo Kisen Kaisha shipping line, the crate weighed 275 kg. This was because Sparks was himself inside it.

The ship set sail on 2nd January 1923, with Sparks stowed in a fairly accessible place, where he remained hidden for five days, until he got lonely and gave himself up. The following day he was landed in Honolulu and transferred to the city gaol as a stowaway. Sparks denied the suggestion, with some justice. He had, he claimed, accurately described the contents of the box as 'personal effects' and met all due charges on the 'prepaid freight'. The authorities, succumbing to his personal charm and the logic of his arguments, relented and allowed Sparks to remain in Honolulu.

He now resolved to travel on in a boat of his own and went back to his old trade so as to save the money. He bought a condemned and badly corroded metal lifeboat, which he named *Dauntless*, and began to fit her out. Stopping the *Dauntless* from leaking proved daunting, so much so that Sparks gave up the attempt. True to his name he set fire to the hopeless tub and sent her blazing out to sea in the Northeast Trade Winds. Then, after a spell of watching Japanese deep-sea fishermen building auxiliary sampans in the boatyards of Honolulu, Sparks knuckled down and, drawing on observation, inventiveness and a bottomless well of inexperience, built another *Dauntless*. Descriptions of this vessel, which combined various features of light American V-bottom sailing boats and of Japanese auxiliary sampans, appeared in two issues of *Yachting* magazine, the flabbergasted correspondents barely concealing their amazement. Among other strange elements of construction was a cockpit measuring 0.7 x 1 metre in which Sparks reportedly sat "with a canvas apron tight around his waist and stretched to the coaming so as to make it practically watertight".

Having been coached in the rudiments of navigation by friendly seamen, Ira Sparks departed westward, without sextant or chronometer, on 9th January 1924, confident of reaching land as long as he sailed into the setting sun. Ten days out of Honolulu he was spotted by a Japanese fisherman 480 km southwest of Oahu. On 26th March he reached the east coast of Mindanao, in the Philippines, and headed north around the island so as to make for Singapore. But while the boat had sailed the Pacific quite happily with a following wind, she was quite useless at beating against the wind. Sparks therefore had to put about and sail south of Mindanao. From his port of call at Malabang, he sent a letter to a friend, in which he confessed: "I would make a few changes if I was going to make another trip across – two masts, a much longer boat and more keel. This boat turns too quickly and, by having two masts and square rigged, I am sure more pleasure and speed would be had".

By this time, 5th April, the Southwest Monsoon had set in, creating hazards amongst the reefs and channels of the Philippines, a region prickling with pirates at the best of times. Not long after, *Dauntless* was found near Zamboanga, on the southwestern tip of Mindanao, unmanned and stripped of all equipment and gear. She was hauled into the harbour while a search was made for the owner, and eventually broken up. Ira Sparks was never seen or heard from again – not a single word, and certainly not The Word, which in due course was carried to India by more reliable means.

The Call of the Bluff

In treasure hunting, rumour and greed are powerful stimuli.

Two partners heard whispers that Spanish silver was buried in the side of a bluff in a remote area of Texas. They leased 8,000 hectares of the surrounding land, hired equipment including an oil drilling rig and began punching holes in the top of the bluff to depths of fifteen metres. Had they prefaced their search with less than an hour's proper research, they would have known at the outset what they discovered at the end: that there was no silver there and never had been.

Worse still was the time when rumour lured three separate groups of treasure seekers into a fruitless search for a fortune supposedly hidden in a cave near Calixico, Mexico. All of them endowed with more time and money than sense, they wasted enormous sums and energies in cutting roads to the site, bulldozing huge tracts of land, dynamiting rock and slicing away one end of the hill. The local people knew where the cave was (covered a few years earlier by a landslide) and its contents (nil), but nobody asked them. So the cave remained undisturbed, where it had always been – on the *other* side of the hill.

TAKING FLIGHT IN YOSEMITE

"Ranger Dick Martin" reported Legal Officer Scott Connelly of the Yosemite Law Enforcement Office "advised that he had placed the defendant [Robin Heid] under arrest for attempting to parachute off El Capitan Mountain, at which time the defendant ran and jumped off the cliff and parachuted to the ground in an unlawful flight to avoid prosecution."

Would anybody actually parachute off El Capitan in order to avoid prosecution? No. But the enforcers of Yosemite have a way of seeing human behaviour through crime-tinted spectacles.

El Capitan has been called the most sublime feature of California's Yosemite Valley. Huge crack systems and vast blank faces of smooth rock pattern the multi-coloured granite of this towering monolith. For years, climbers have considered El Capitan the world's ultimate big wall.

But Heid and his companions did not go to Yosemite to climb this cliff. They were going to step from its edge and fly past it.

Robin Heid takes up the story:

"The hike up the rear side of the mountain was strenuous. Loaded with packs of camping gear weighing over 20 kg, parachute rigs and half a dozen cameras, we first moved down an abandoned fire road, then up a steep footpath, down again through glades of delicate wild flowers, then up once more into ancient forests of towering, moss-covered sequoias. It was a place of exquisite contrasts.

During one of our frequent rest stops, a pair of climbers passed us by, heading for the summit where they said they expected to meet a couple of friends who were climbing the face. Obviously in enviable shape, they went on up the trail at a sprightly pace.

We crossed a dry stream bed and climbed steeply.

Bare granite began to appear: the summit must be close. Overhead, an Alouette Six helicopter wafted by.

"I wonder where they're going?" mused Jim.

"Probably some kind of rescue", I speculated. "They use Alouettes in Denver for that".

When we reached the summit, we dropped our gear, then picked our way through jumbled sloping boulders in search of the launch point on the Dawn Wall, marked by a metre-high cairn. We found it quickly and looked over the edge. The view from the crown of El Capitan was glorious. After a brief radio check with Mike and Larry in the valley, Jim, Charlie, Jeff, Mike and I headed back to the summit. The twosome we'd met earlier, Hal and Paul, were there too and we invited them to watch us the next day. They seemed very interested and agreed.

We went to bed early so we could start at dawn. Jim was to hike back down the mountain after filming our launches. Alive with anticipation, we made our way to the edge, checked in with Mike, then climbed into our jumpsuits and strapped on our rigs. We proceeded methodically, making sure everything was right — and that we got photographs. Hal was there as well, snapping away with a pocket camera.

"Give your address to Jim, so we can get copies, OK?" asked Charlie.

"Sure" replied Hal.

Suddenly, about ten park rangers popped up simultaneously from behind several large boulders, their positions describing a sort of semicircle around us.

"Alright, boys" shouted one. "The game's over. You're coming with us."

One ranger began a flanking movement on the sloping rock to get between us and the lip of the 800-metre-high precipice. He grinned.

"Now I don't want you boys getting any ideas" he said.

Jeff and Charlie didn't move, but I stepped sideways

and skipped over to the cairn. The ranger froze and the grin vanished as he realised how close he was to the edge. I looked at Jim, who was leaning on the cairn with a movie camera, fastened my helmet and gave my gear a final check.

"Got the camera ready?" I asked.

"Yes. Are *you* ready?"

"Yeah, I'm ready".

"Don't do anything stupid, Robin" said Charlie.

"Under control" I replied.

The rangers watched in stunned silence; this was not part of their plan. For a moment they seemed to have forgotten why we were there at the edge of El Capitan in the first place. Finally one of them spoke.

"Don't jump".

I ignored him and caught Jim's eye again.

"Ready?"

He nodded.

"You ready?"

"Ready." I gazed at the stern-faced men before me, bowed slightly from the waist and straightened up.

"You gentlemen have a nice day" I said with a smile.

Then I turned to my left and ran off the edge with a hearty "Yahoo!"

Now there was only the sublimity of El Capitan and the joy of flying, as I accelerated valleyward in the delicious rush of wind and motion that is free flight. Granite blurred behind me, the scree at the foot of the monolith expanded as I dived. It was a moment suspended in sensory time. After ten seconds I deployed my canopy; when it blossomed overhead, I turned in a gentle sweeping arc, absorbing the majesty of the valley. A warm sweet feeling permeated my body and spirit. A bubble of energy rose inside me and burst from my throat as a whoop of delight.

Shortlived ecstasy: below me, the rangers were waiting. To avoid being spotted I put down in an open space in a forest of massive conifers, shed my gear quickly, stuffed it in a bag and stashed it under a pile of brush.

Thinking I should warn Mike and Larry, I jogged toward the campground. When I reached their car I found the place swarming with rangers. I should have known; in so well-coordinated a raid, they'd have the bottom covered as well. The rangers escorted me to the Enforcement Compound – I looked 'suspiciously like' someone they wanted for questioning, they said.

Still, I thought, they'd have no way of positively identifying me for several hours – until the force on top of El Capitan returned to base. I might still get away with it.

Then a ranger walked over and asked me to show him what I was wearing under my sweatshirt. "The guy we're looking for is wearing a blue T-shirt with the motto 'Disco Sucks' ". The rangers chuckled happily as I revealed the guilty garment. I was puzzled. I'd had my jumpsuit on by the time the rangers at the top saw me . . .

"Wonderin' how we knew that, huh?", sniggered one. "Well, those two quote-unquote 'climbers' were actually rangers. Hope you won't be too mad at them – they were only doing their job . . ."

I wasn't angry, just amazed. And I started thinking about those immaculately uniformed rangers who had accosted us at the edge.

"Did you use that chopper to bring people in yesterday?" I asked the happy ranger. His face lit up. He was eager to tell me the whole plan now that the "game" was over.

"You bet. They stayed up there all night. Hell, a couple of them were so close one of you guys almost took a leak on them!"

"How much does it cost per hour to run your Alouette?"

A frown. "I don't know".

I was now under 'custodial arrest'. I was stripped,

searched, fingerprinted, photographed and gaoled. My little belt knife, less than eight centimetres long, got me into further trouble. The entry next to my name in the arrest log was altered from M for misdemeanour to F for felony when it was discovered. "Carrying a dagger is a felony" Connelly explained. In California, apparently, any knife with a double edge is considered a deadly weapon. As I don't live in California, how was I to know that?

Within a few hours, my companions were brought into gaol too. The interrogations began. One by one we were ushered into the Legal Officer's presence. Jeff was accused of 'stealing government property' because several of his 16mm cine cameras were World War II fighter plane gun cameras – readily available on the surplus market. There were veiled threats and crass attempts to bargain in return for 'cooperation'.

The cells were wired for sound. The ranger who had scared himself on top of the mountain was feeling much braver now. "Are *you* having a nice day?" he jeered, as he sauntered past at one point. "*I'm* having a nice day".

When we went to see the magistrate, we were handcuffed and locked in prison trucks. Our alleged crimes were described to the magistrate. It seemed we had contravened a regulation listed in the 36 Code of Federal Regulations:

'2.2 Aircraft

(a) The operation or use of aircraft on lands or waters other than at the landing areas designated in special regulations is prohibited . . .

(b) Except in extreme emergencies involving the safety of human life or threat of serious property loss, the air delivery of any person or thing by parachute, helicopter or other means without prior written permission is prohibited.'

Exceptions are also permitted for aircraft on official government business or landings forced by circumstances beyond the operator's control.

As the only one who jumped, I got special attention in the form of the allegations mentioned at the beginning.

We pleaded not guilty, of course, and, after a two-hour lunch adjournment by the magistrate the court reconvened and everyone except me was released on their own recognisance. Since I had 'attempted to avoid prosecution' and was, therefore, a more desperate criminal, I was forced to post a $300 cash bail. The magistrate and the Legal Officer, agreeing that 'evidence' was required for the case, confiscated over $12,000 worth of parachute equipment and photographic gear from us, including a hired camera for which Jeff was paying about $25 a day. When he protested, he was told to shut up.

After additional delays and harassment, we were finally released. At least, we thought so.

We had barely cleared the gates of the Enforcement Compound when a pack of rangers pursued us again. They stopped us, ordered us from our vehicles and searched our bodies and possessions once again. They refused to say why, only muttering darkly about 'felony conspiracy'. Mike was rearrested for something like 'contributing to the disappearance of government property' and hauled back to gaol. The rest of us were released for what we hoped would be the last time.

Jeff stayed behind to make sure the others had transport. Jim and I, deciding that we'd had enough, hitched a lift and were outside the gates of Yosemite very shortly after."

Readers who have difficulty believing that such treatment can be meted out to sportsmen and adventurers in the Land of the Free should remember that George Willig was arrested after climbing the outside walls of the World Trade Center, New York City, and Philippe Petit for walking the high wire between the twin towers of the same building. Chopping your mother up in Massachusetts is only one of many things forbidden under U.S.

law. In Canada, Miri Ercolani, aged 54, attempted to repeat a route first traversed by the Duke of Abruzzi on Mt. St. Elias. The Canadians, acting in accordance with a regulation which effectively bans solo climbing in the St. Elias area, forcibly removed her from the mountain by helicopter. Undeterred – which is as it should be – she went on to solo Mt. McKinley in Alaska.

Take a Partner
Housewife magazine ran a competition once on 'How I met my husband'. The winner had bumped into her future husband while canoeing in thick fog. Reporting on this in January 1950, *The Canoe-Camper* magazine cautioned: 'We cannot advise our unmarried members to *depend* upon this method'.

CHARACTERS

. . . as large as life, and twice as natural!
– Lewis Carroll, The Walrus and the Carpenter,
Through the Looking Glass.

LEGENDS IN THEIR OWN LIFELINES

By ordinary standards, the Dangerous Sports Club of Oxford are, as Lady Caroline Lamb said of Byron, 'mad, bad and dangerous to know'. Public knowledge and approval are some way down their list of priorities, and as long as they can pursue their inclinations unharassed and uncensured they are fairly content to remain also unhonoured and unsung.

The DSC came into being as a channel through which to escape 'the boredom of plastic pressurised everyday living'. Elegance and dash are their trademarks; formal dress – top hats, tails and a Club tie that rather tastelessly carries a motif of a man in a wheelchair – their uniform; and a blend of inventive novelty with the ancient British tradition of amateurism their mode of operation. Like Percy Bysshe Shelley's skylark, they aim to display 'fine, careless rapture', accompanied by an air of secure and confident control; but unlike that of the blithe spirit in the poem, their art is anything but premeditated. Calculations of stresses and strains are routine for them, but they have no time for the elitism and exclusivity of many sporting establishments, substituting cool brain-work and common sense for regulation, tuition and 'proper' ways of acquiring skills. "The question", says one of their number, Tim Hunt, "is not whether you have the technical knowledge to do what you intend. It is just a matter of wanting to do it. It's that simple."

114

Willingly, they are debunkers of one set of myths; unwittingly, they are purveyors of another set.

The conspiracy of fun is run by a hard core of part-time intellectuals associated one way or another with Oxford's academe. At the centre are David Kirke, a lecturer in his mid-thirties, thinning somewhat on top and thickening somewhat in the middle; Ed Hulton, a millionaire who now lives in tax exile in Monaco; and Chris Hiatt-Baker, son of a wealthy land-owner. Many of the ring-leaders are, indeed, sons, daughters and brothers of the rich and famous, though the Club professes a splendid disregard for money, class or social status. *All* Westerners are privileged vis-à-vis much of the rest of the world, they say, and have a responsibility to use their advantaged position to act boldly in a 'timorous, over-protected world'. Nevertheless, the Club is very select in its way. Membership is usually by invitation of Mr Kirke, and 'once you've refused, you're not invited again'. The DSC is no place for the indecisive. Nor, to face facts, for the impecunious: Club activities to date have been largely self-financed.

There is an uneasy relationship between Club members and society, particularly its wielders of authority. This is not unusual: most developed societies like to maintain law and order, even at the expense of what Kirke calls 'life-questioning sport'. As Robin Heid, an American adventurer, puts it: "A stimulated populace is a threat to the state", and anyone willing to go so far as 'to die other than in defence of his country is seen as a threat to it'. On the whole, it is society's business to say 'no' to non-conformity. And on the whole, it is Kirke and Co.s business to say 'yes'. But there is room for concessions. When the Club members performed one of their 'sports' on the Golden Gate Bridge in San Francisco, Kirke wrote an open letter of appeasement to the officers who would, as sure as fate, arrest them. It is typical of their arcane, yet rather graceful, style. "We would ask you not to be alarmed. With the possible exception of the jumpers, nobody is subject to the slightest danger or inconvenience and there is no reason why one should not proceed about one's daily business. . . . A fine etiquette should be observed".

This delivered, they donned formal wear, and harnesses and, attached to the railing by an elasticated rope apiece known as a bungy, they leaped over the side, bounced several times and came to a standstill about halfway between bridge and ocean.

The Dangerous Sports Club first made itself manifest by holding an 'At Home' on top of Rockall, Britain's tiny and sheer-sided rock dominion in the Atlantic. Present were the three above-mentioned hosts and no guests, none having been invited. Nevertheless, the event commanded much of the aura of a conventionally sophisticated party, with black tie and tails, champagne and oysters, music by Wagner and a dive into the sea afterwards.

Clinging still in their days of infancy to the security of 'ordinary' sports, the Club
- hang-glided from the summits of Mts. Kilimanjaro, Olympus and Etna;
- skateboarded in front of the bulls in Pamplona;
- had dinner of sulphur-speckled chicken salad and ash-tainted wine off a white (but not for long) tablecloth on the lip of the Soufrière volcano on the Caribbean island of St. Vincent;
- went down the bobsleigh run at St. Moritz, Switzerland, in a London taxi and atop a block of ice fitted with a seat;
- climbed the Matterhorn with little equipment and less expertise;
- launched themselves down the treacherous white water of the Landquart river in Austria; and
- flew an aeroplane without any experience or training whatever.

Then, apparently tiring of the relative tameness of such conventional pursuits, they began to invent their own sports.

Prime among these is the sport of bungy jumping, an urban version of the vine jumping practised by the natives of New Guinea, who leap from trees with vines tied to their ankles. Their first display of this exercise was on April Fool's Day 1979, when Kirke and three others jumped from the Clifton Suspension Bridge in Bristol. Public notice was attracted, to the feigned confusion of Kirke, who murmured: "I don't know what all the fuss was about. We just wanted to get away somewhere on our own for a little peace and quiet to discuss politics and things like that. This was the ideal place." Despite putting in what he described as an 'undignified' performance and accidentally dropping into the river the bottle of champagne with which he had hoped to celebrate the event, Kirke attested that it had been "a wonderful experience". And to prove it, he and other members and associates of the Club have since bungy-jumped from the Golden Gate Bridge, as mentioned, from the Royal Gorge, the world's highest suspension bridge, 320 metres above the Arkansas River in the Rocky Mountains of Colorado (to the accompaniment of music played by Hubert Gibbs, the group's 'official pianist', on a rented instrument), and from a balloon. Like many unorthodox adventurers the DSC members habitually brush with the police, usually on charges such as trespassing, breach of the peace and other 'crimes', and respond to this necessary evil with true sportsmanship.

Other recent DSC adventures have been just as startling:

In May 1980, Kirke, Jack McCornack from the USA and a commodities broker by the name of John Leigh-Pemberton attempted to fly powered hang-gliders called Pterodactyls from Croydon to Paris. None of them got as far as the British side of the Channel. Bad visibility and strong winds forced two of the pilots to make emergency landings. Kirke had only reached Tatsfield in Surrey when he began to lose height, or, as he put it, "the countryside started gaining height". After another abortive start, he made a 26-point crash landing in a tree, where, with his customary insouciance, he lit a cigar and delivered himself of the opinion that he had been 'nobbled'. "There I was whizzing round the sky like an inebriated bumble bee," he said, "while my friends were arrogantly waving goodbye". McCornack made light of his failure. "I don't even like Paris", he said. In October of the same year, Kirke made it across to Paris in six hours, setting a new distance record of 384 km with his fabric and aluminium hang-glider and breaking every rule in the book on this strictly illegal flight. Kirke's companion, Philip Oppenheim, managed on this occasion not even to get his Pterodactyl airborne, though subsequently he became the first to fly such a machine from Land's End to John O'Groats, a distance of 1,360 km.

An attempt by the Club to cross the Channel suspended underneath balloons, from Beachy Head to France, failed (Christmas 1980) when cold cracked the plastic of the balloons and the gas escaped.

In August 1982, a Dangerously Sporting Clubman, dressed in a gorilla suit and playing a saxophone, 'buzzed' the Houses of Parliament in a powered hang-glider, demonstrating the laxity of security arrangements in that august domain and zipping off to France, via Epping, before the police could draw him into discussion.

Tenuously connected with the world of sport was a project of Ed Hulton's. Obsessed with the idea of keeping an historic aircraft out of a museum, and blessed with the funds to feed the notion, he bought the world's only airworthy Sunderland flying boat, a 38-year-old specimen of the type used against U-boats, and before putting her on show in London to raise money for the South Atlantic Fund (1982 Falklands campaign), refurbished her at a cost of about £1 million.

Ever game for a laugh, the Dangerous Sports Club have plenty more capers and fancies up their collective sleeve, amongst them the idea of hang-gliding off Mt. Everest – even if they have to 'charter a helicopter to the summit'. But members are wary of disclosing their plans in advance; knowing that they can count on trouble after the event, they don't look for it before as well.

There is risk involved, sometimes considerable risk. The Golden Gate Bridge bungy jump offered, for example, only a two per cent safety margin. At the Royal Gorge, Kirke, attached to a 130-metre cord which stretched out to twice its length as he fell, started tumbling upside down. "If the bungy had caught when I was in that position then I was a certain gonner", he said. With a force of eight Gs (the force of gravity), he came to a halt and nearly passed out, to be hauled up after dangling for two and a quarter hours in below-freezing temperatures. Dangerous, indeed, but psychologically speaking a safety valve. "Everyone has a certain level of anxiety. I direct my anxiety into the events I attempt. The rest of my life is very calm". And it is with calmness that the Club accept the risks. "Every event may be my last", Kirke concedes. "Festivity is required. If anything goes wrong, the party must celebrate life, not mourn death". Easier said than done, if put to the test, but so far the Club has managed to stay on the right side of tragedy.

Meanwhile, they continue to cherish what T.S. Eliot, in his poem *The Wasteland*, called 'the ecstasy of a moment's surrender, which a lifetime of prudence can never undo".

JAPANESE EXPERTISE OUT IN FRONT

"These expeditions might have no social value in themselves," confesses Naomi Uemura, "but there is something that drives me to do them". Whatever it is, it isn't science.

119

The 42-year-old Japanese has a number of unique claims to fame, not least of which is the rare frankness with which he describes himself as an adventurer, not an explorer.

Uemura specialises in solo 'firsts' and 'longests'. Between 1966 and 1970 he became the first man to climb the highest mountain on five continents: Mt. Blanc, Kilimanjaro, McKinley, Aconcagua and Everest. All, except the last, alone. He once piloted a small balsa raft down the entire 6,100-km length of the Amazon River. Between December 1974 and May 1976 he established a new Arctic record by completing the longest recorded solo dog-sled journey. Like the Dane, Knud Rasmussen, fifty years earlier, Uemura traversed Greenland and northern Canada to Kotzebue, Alaska, a journey of 12,000 km. Unlike Rasmussen, Uemura did it alone.

In May 1978 Uemura became the first person to reach the North Pole singlehanded. He had started in March from Ellesmere Island in the Canadian Arctic, in a sled named *Aurora* drawn by seventeen huskies. Three days out, a marauding polar bear invaded his tent, ate all his food and would have moved on to Uemura himself, had he not had the good sense to keep perfectly still until the bear moved away. When the great beast returned the next day, Uemura killed it and calmly arranged for fresh food supplies to be flown in. In temperatures below −40C, the adventurer hacked his way through an almost endless labyrinth of jagged ice ridges and boulders. Blizzards swept through to hamper his progress. At one point the ice cap fractured, trapping Uemura on an 84 sq. m ice floe, until the ice rejoined the pack and froze back in place. When one of his huskies gave birth to six puppies, he had to stay put until they could be collected and flown back to base camp.

His arrival at the Pole, four days after a team of students from Tokyo's Nihon University, was notified at the Smithsonian Institute in Washington through an automatic 'bleeper' carried by the adventurer and relayed by an American satellite. Uemura's trials were now only half over: he still had to cover about as far again (c. 750 km), travelling the length of Greenland to journey's end at Narsarssuak, near its southern tip.

Like most people, Uemura likes to achieve his objects. But, more than that, he loves to 'have a dream and then one day make it real'. The true success is to begin.

Try, Try Again
Early in 1983, Englishman David Hempleman-Adams also attempted to reach the North Pole alone. He travelled on foot and on skis, without dogs, and allowed himself only four air drops in 38 days (a drop was made to Uemura every other day). His budget for the journey came to about £35,000, as against Uemura's price tag of about £2 million. When the weather and a broken rib bullied him into retreat, Hempleman-Adams gave up gracefully, saying he'd rather be a live failure than a dead hero. Unlike the latter, live failures have the option of trying again, which is what the young 'professional adventurer' vowed to do.

THE HAPPINESS-MAKER

'Art is the contemplation of the world independently of the principle of reason'
– Schopenhauer

"I don't know. I can't explain. There is no why". So said Philippe Petit of his compulsion to walk tightropes. "When I see three oranges I want to juggle. When I see two towers I want to walk".

This much he does know: "the other stuff" – the death-defying activity of such as motorcycle jumper Evel Knievel – "is stunt. I am art."

He is also, in the opinion of the forces of law and order, crafty, crazy and criminal.

Philippe Petit, whose 163 cm stature matches his name, was born in 1949 in Nemours, France, the son of an Army colonel. Naturally lithe and nimble, he taught himself the carnival arts – magic, juggling, horseback acrobatics, riding a unicycle and tightrope-walking – before dropping out of school at the age of fifteen and vagabonding around France 'like a strolling player in the Middle Ages', entertaining street crowds and living hand to mouth. More and more he came to love the wire and learned 'to put wires imaginatively everywhere'. The two belfries of the Cathedral of Notre Dame in Paris were inviting targets.

One night in June 1971, Philippe and some accomplices secreted themselves inside the Cathedral (with the help of keys duplicated surreptitiously). They secured a wire by throwing a ball with a fishline attached from one tower to the other. In the morning, at ten o'clock, the tower doors opened to the first of the morning tourists. A moment later Petit stepped out onto the wire. Seventy metres above the ground, before a gathering audience that eventually numbered thousands, he walked, ran and juggled on the wire. Unbeknown to him, fifty priests were at this time being ordained in the great nave of the Cathedral. The bells of Notre Dame pealing out at the conclusion of the ceremony startled Petit, who was at that moment lying down on the cable. "It was ironic", he remarked. "The fifty priests, dressed in white vest-ments, were lying prostrate, facing hell. And I, dressed in black, was looking at heaven".

The show ended with Petit, exhausted but triumphant, running into the arms of the police, who led him away, to the cheers of the multitude. "The people running after me in excitement was the most beautiful thing I have ever seen", said Philippe, who is as given to overstatement as he is to overactivity. "It was a revolution of happiness!" The authorities at Notre Dame showed praiseworthy restraint. "That was not a crime, it was an exploit", declared the Cathedral's curator. "Let him go".

Like the priests, Petit was ordained to go on to greater things. The world, to anyone with an eye for it, is full of towers – towers with huge blank spaces hanging between them. Invited to perform in Australia, Petit walked a wire between the pylons of the Sydney Harbour Bridge in 1973.

And then came the World Trade Center, 110 stories and 412 metres high, the greatest of New York City's modern landmarks and the second-tallest building in the world. Standing on wire-laced steel foundations twenty metres deep, the building contains 690,000 square metres of office space. The lobbies are seven stories high and the Center is served by 208 escalators. To Petit, one fact was paramount: *twin towers.*

His first look at the still incomplete structure left him with two contradictory convictions: "I concentrate on the void that separates the two towers. The space is too big, an enormous emptiness where one wouldn't dare to venture . . . It's impossible. But I know that I will do it".

Early in 1974, Petit took up residence in downtown Manhattan with the express purpose of bringing off the impossible. "I will become the emperor of the sky", he told his friends. In the United States, with its democratic system of 'checks and balances', the provision made for emperors is negligible and Petit knew that his balancing act was likely to be severely checked. That he would fall foul of the law was crystal-clear from the outset, though which law was anybody's guess. "He should have asked permission first", a press officer of the New York Port Authority said later. Would he have been given permission? "Never", she replied.

For six months, Petit and his friends plotted and planned – posing as correspondents for an architectural journal, as delivery men, as construction workers in overalls and hard hats; riding elevators, climbing staircases, exploring, photographing and questioning; forging alliances with reliable American recruits who could obtain inside information about the security and structure of the building; finding a hideout and bit by bit transporting 270 kg of equipment to a place near the top of the North Tower where it could be hidden among building materials. In all, they stored seventy metres of 21-ply galvanised steel cable 2.2 cm wide and weighing 120 kg, a winch for tightening it, other cable for guy wires to support and steady the main performing cable, a one-and-a-half-metre crossbow for firing the wire from the North to the South Tower, pulleys and block-and-tackle units, Petit's ten-metre balancing rod (jointed at three places for easier handling) and a wheeled suitcase containing tools, metal fittings, shackles and clamps. An intercom system was rigged up for communication between the two towers. Petit and his colleague and helper Jean-François Heckel positioned themselves in readiness on the night of 6–7th August 1974 on the South Tower; a French photographer friend, accompanied by an American, would be on the North Tower, responsible for securing the main wire. The night's accommodation – on a beam in a lift-shaft – was uncomfortable in the extreme, but nothing compared with the pain and exertion of hauling in the wire, tautening it and attaching the steel guy lines.

By now it was 6 am, and Petit had to make a start before the workers arrived for the day. Though faint from exhaustion and trembling with fatigue, he had no alternative but to go on. He had already looked the project straight in the eye: "There is a 50-50 chance the feat will succeed. The guards, the wind, the wire, me . . .

I am cold with fear and frozen with happiness". It was time to step out.

Concentrating hard on the opposite tower, conjuring up all his reserves of determination, he crossed in measured footsteps over the forty-metre length of cable to the other side. A check of the wires and he was on his way back again, redoubled confidence giving him spring and energy. Suddenly he started to enjoy himself. "I couldn't help laughing – it was so beautiful". Four hundred metres below, on the ground, New York's early birds began to collect to watch the spectacle. Traffic on the Brooklyn Bridge came to a halt. "New York woke up and what did it discover?" recalled Petit later in his picturesque English. "There was a high walker on the twin towers. I was not scared because it was a precise thing. I was happy. I was dying of happiness".

A World Trade Center guard alerted the police, but had to repeat his call several times before anyone would believe him. At last, at 7.30 am, Port Authority Police Sgt. Charles Daniels put into effect *Emergency Jump Plan* (for suicides) in order to prevent Petit from dying of anything other than happiness – or indeed from falling on top of someone else and causing a double death. "Not that we ever expected to use the plan," said Daniels, "but we have contingency plans for everything". Realising that the men could frighten Petit and literally precipitate a fall, Daniels tried persuasion: a helicopter would come and pluck Petit off the wire, Daniels warned in his schoolboy French.

Meanwhile, Petit remained on the wire, and Daniels watched, awestruck, for some forty minutes. "I figured I was watching something no-one else would ever see again", said the sergeant. Petit danced, jumped, bowed from the waist to the crowd, lay down on the wire and rolled about with the pole resting on his stomach, and dropped to one knee in the traditional salute of the tightrope walker. The sight of the police inspired him to a manoeuvre he had never performed perfectly before, even in practice: he 'executed a turnaround, placing the balancing pole on the wire, whirling around and picking it up again'. In all, he made seven crossings between the towers, with only one bad moment when the commotion made him lose concentration and stumble.

Of the thousands who watched and applauded the artist's every move, there were a few who couldn't stay the course. A chef in a local coffee shop peeped up but soon scuttled back indoors. "My stomach gave out" he explained . . . and I had breakfast to cook".

After what he described as "the most beautiful crossing", Philippe Petit decided to end the performance on a high note. He ran along the wire and leapt onto the roof of the tower. The police broke into applause – and then arrested him, capture following rapture.

On the opposite tower, the two accomplices made a getaway as soon as the police appeared. First stop for handcuffed 'prisoners' Petit and Heckel was the psychiatric ward at Beekman Downtown Hospital, where a spokesman pronounced them both "in excellent health physically and psychologically", though adding the rider: "They seem like perfectly normal people. But anyone who does this 110 storeys up can't be entirely right." Then came a trip to the First Precinct police station in Lower Manhattan where Sgt. Daniels deliberated over appropriate charges, while Petit amused himself and assorted photographers by balancing a policeman's cap on his nose and flipping it onto his head. Finally, the police charged Petit and Heckel with criminal trespass and disorderly conduct. The District Attorney, exercising both his discretion and his imagination, persuaded the judge to drop the charges on condition that Petit put on a show for the children of New York. A unique 'crime' warranted a unique penalty, and accordingly, one evening three weeks later, Petit took his high-wire act to Central Park and walked barefoot along a 200-metre cable stretched across Belvedere Lake. Five thousand spectators (some of whom *were* children) watched him ascend the thirty-degree wire strung more than twenty metres in the air. Standing discreetly by were three orange-suited city lifeguards: Petit had seemed a little concerned about being unable to swim. A park employee foresaw another danger: the water is only two metres deep, he explained, "but if he falls in, he'd be killed by all the broken glass at the bottom".

The exploit which Petit said was "the craziest thing I did in my life" was redeemed through 'the greatest event that has ever come to the City of New York'. With his escapade at the World Trade Center, Petit had almost doubled the previous world record for high-wire walking, established over the 23-metre-deep Tallulah Gorge in Georgia by Karl Wallenda in 1970 (Petit's record still stands) – not to mention bringing joy to a troubled nation. Newspapers, anticipating the abdication of the nation's President after the Watergate scandal, headlined the Petit story *Another Man on a Tightrope*. While one man's failure clouded the American skies, the other's success made good his boast that he would "walk across the top of New York for happiness". Although the attendant fame came with the usual trimmings, such as money, Petit insisted he didn't need anything. "When you are full of fire" he said "you can move mountains. When you give everything to your art, you become transformed". Among his dreams: to walk directly over the Niagara Falls (not as his compatriot Blondin did it, slightly downriver, in 1859); to suspend a cable to the top of the Eiffel Tower and walk up at a 45-degree angle; in short, to strive constantly for perfection – *petit' chose*, just a little thing, like himself.

The Skiing Tuareg

Hadji Abderrahmane, a Tuareg originally from the village of Adriane near Tamanrasset, is the proprietor of a café and campsite in In Salah in southern Algeria. In Salah is a major watering, refuelling and rest point along the main trans-Saharan *piste*. Since opening his Café-Restaurant du Carrefour there in 1973, Hadji has come into contact with most subsequent trans-Saharan travellers. Motivated by pure kindness and an insatiable interest in Western ways, he has been an angel of mercy to countless people who have ventured into the desert ill-prepared or who have met with bad luck. When, as happens frequently, he travels abroad – invariably clad in his traditional robes and headdress – he can be assured of a warm welcome and comfortable lodging in any European city.

M. Abderrahmane is also a bit of an extravert and loves publicity. In 1980, after a trip to Switzerland, he returned to In Salah with a pair of skis and proceeded to demonstrate to German and Austrian journalists his skill in skiing among the sand dunes. Photos of him on skis and wearing sunglasses together with his usual voluminous robes appeared in various European magazines. In 'The Skiing Tuareg', In Salah has acquired yet another irresistible attraction for Saharan travellers.

MAGNUM FORBES

"A balloon is not meant to be tied down. It is a beautiful thing to see if you are not the minister of foreign affairs." So said Malcolm Forbes during his visit to China in

October 1982 when he often found himself entangled in red tape. He might have added "or if you are not a small-town Chinese". Most of those had never seen a balloon before and took his 22-metre-tall specimen for some kind of satellite.

Forbes, 63-year-old American adventurer, self-publicist and publisher of a magazine that bears his name and advertises itself as 'the capitalist tool', was in China breaking rules, entertaining his hosts and having a ball.

His visit was arranged by the industrialist Armand Hammer, who obtained the personal approval of the Chinese leader, Deng Xiaoping himself, for Forbes' tour. In two and a half weeks, Forbes caused a minor riot wherever he went, but a sense of humour on both sides and what the Chinese call *guanxi* – connections – smoothed ruffled feathers.

Malcolm Forbes and his five American companions arrived in China on 5th October and headed for Xian in the centre of the country. During a ballooning demonstration he arranged at a sports stadium there, he put his foot wrong for the first time. Forbes and several assistants rose into the air – and over the stadium wall. Frantic calls over the walkie-talkie begged them to come down at once. Forbes tried to explain that landing a balloon is not as easy as taking off in one, and proved it minutes later by crashing into the top of an unmortared brick wall, causing a little damage to the gondola and a bit more to the wall, on the way to a distinctly bumpy landing in a nearby field.

Three days later the Forbes team, dressed in black motorcycle leathers and red leather vests, set off with the multicoloured balloon and five identical motorcycles for a tour across central China. In twelve days, they zigzagged 2,400 km, sleeping in hotels where they could and in tents where they couldn't. They passed through areas seldom seen by foreigners, where the locals thought the Harley Davidsons were atomic weapons of some sort – a fear magnified by the escort of police vehicles that, with sirens shrieking, preceded the Forbes party all the way.

In Beijing, which they reached on 19th October, Forbes obligingly attended banquets and a news conference, and impulsively fixed up a midnight meeting with Pakistan's President Zia, himself on a visit to China.

Early next morning, Forbes' fleet of motorcycles thundered out to the Great Wall to try a balloon flight. The Beijing authorities, having heard what had happened in Xian, were now suffering from balloon fright, and forbade Forbes to untie the tether. Forbes took this obstacle in his leather-booted stride and roared back to Beijing. "Maybe tomorrow" he told a reporter who, barely suppressing his terror, was trying to interview him from the back of his motorcycle.

The next day, Forbes inflated the balloon for a group of athletes at a stadium outside Beijing and gave them rides up to the length of the tether and down again. When it came the turn of China's champion javelin thrower to climb into the gondola, Forbes' mischievous instincts got the better of him. Glancing down at the security men below, he untied the tether and began to drift up and away. Shouts of "No free flight! No free flight!" came up to him. But Forbes, for whom the word 'no' is always sufficient encouragement to go ahead, was enjoying himself, and so, after the initial shock, was his passenger.

About fifteen minutes later, Forbes landed the balloon. "I don't know where we are," he reported over a crackly walkie-talkie, "but there are cannons pointed at us." And immediately he was surrounded by delighted soldiers. The commander of the high-security military base in which Forbes had put down was not so pleased. He kept gesticulating at the balloonist to urge him to leave, until he was mollified by the gift of a balloon-shaped commemorative pin and asked to pose for a photo.

Almost anyone else would have been arrested, but Forbes was instead feted at a farewell banquet at the Great Hall of the People later that night. There he created much hilarity with stories of his breaches of the rules during his visit. Revelling in the publicity, Forbes said he hadn't meant to be 'naughty' or 'unfriendly', but had just wanted to demonstrate that 'ballooning is a wonderful sport'. Li Menghua, China's Minister for Physical Culture and Sports, conceded that "Yours was a most impressive visit", and another observer commented that it had been "one of the most surprising visits to China since Marco Polo's".

'All is forgiven' was the Chinese message to their first visiting motorcycle balloonist, 'come back'. But they were careful not to name a date.

HOW THE FAUSSETT GOT TURNED ON

"Dad was another Evel Knievel. He was just born forty years too soon. There wasn't the instant publicity back then to make him rich and famous".

This is the verdict of Irv, son of Al Faussett, daredevil American waterfall jumper of the 1920s.

It all began with Twentieth Century Fox. A film crew was in Washington State to make a western in which one scene called for an Indian to ride over a waterfall in a dugout canoe. The rapids were easy enough to pick – Sunset Falls on Washington's Skykomish River offers a drop of thirty-two metres over an eighty-four-metre diagonal granite slide. Finding someone to jump the falls wasn't so simple, so the studio offered $1,500 to anyone crazy enough to perform the stunt.

Al Faussett, a small-time lumberjack with his own logging business, was the only volunteer. Fox's canoe didn't strike him as suitable, so he decided to make his own. He felled a spruce and hewed a ten-metre canoe from it, adding a sheet metal cowl over the foredeck and a canvas cover aft, and left a small opening in the stern in which he could strap himself in. Vine maple in one-and-a-half-metre lengths were fastened to the hull at various angles. By this stage, the canoe looked so unlike a genuine Indian dugout that Fox withdrew the offer. Faussett and his craft, ready and raring to go, were left high and dry. But an entrepreneurial spirit like Faussett's doesn't just sit back and accept a ruling that says 'Do not collect $1,500. Do not pass GO". With encourage-ment from his friends, Faussett resolved to run the Sunset Falls anyway. The date was set for 30th May 1926 and an admission fee fixed at one dollar.

Since the only thing Faussett feared was fear itself, he was able to assure reporters confidently that he was in for a 'dangerous and thrilling' but a 'cool ride' and would negotiate the falls where twenty men had previously lost their lives.

On the set date, three hours after the advertised time and in front of 3,000 spectators, Faussett's canoe crashed through the falls engulfed in water. It bounced off a large granite outcrop, leapt halfway into the air and slammed back down again, where it disappeared in the foam for several seconds. Then the rider, wearing an inner tube wrapped around his body for a life jacket, emerged from the spray and, from a calm pool, waved to the wildly applauding crowd.

Even fearless Faussett had been surprised by the treacherous force of the waters. "When I went under," he wrote afterwards, "the water hit me with a crushing force and hurt my lungs. It twisted my body and head. I was hurt inside and could not breathe. The water came so fast it crammed down my nostrils and throat.

"At no time was I afraid of those falls, not even when the water seemed to be crushing the very life out of me. It was all over in a few seconds and, when I saw the light of day as I rode out of the turbulent waters, I thanked

God that I had ridden safely through. I have challenged the world to the effect that I can ride anywhere any human can in my good canoe".

Or, to be more accurate, in any canoe of his own devising. In the next three years, Faussett rode five more falls in the Northwest in an assortment of strange craft.

Later in 1926 he ran the Eagle Falls, a short way upriver from Sunset. This time he rode inside the boat, a five-metre cigar-shaped creation made by strapping the hollowed-out halves of a log together, to which he gained access through a trapdoor. He made it to the bottom of the falls alright, though there had been those who doubted whether he'd make it to the top, since the water was so low that day that the boat wedged on the rocks and had to be pushed free with a pike pole.

Faussett wasn't allowed to run the Snoqualmie Falls (sixty-six metres) or even one of the less well known rapids upstream: Puget Power and the Sheriff of King County between them snuffed out these ideas out of concern for their own good and, as they thought, Faussett's too. But like all good adventurers Faussett couldn't be deterred, even though he might be diverted. He would go elsewhere – to the Spokane Falls. The Spokane chief of police decided to give Faussett his head but refused him the right to charge for admission. Accordingly, half the city's population turned up to watch the free spectacle on 3rd June 1927.

The boat, similar to that used on the Eagle Falls, weighed 352 kg, but the river treated it like matchwood, rushing it towards the lip of the twenty-three-metre staircase cataract. Over the first step the boat somersaulted; then it was sucked into a whirlpool where it spun around for over twenty minutes until at last it swept within reach of men on the river bank who pulled it in. Faussett, concussed, cut and bruised and with blood dripping over his face, staggered out of the boat and straight into a waiting ambulance. "Those falls", he said, "have got whiskers on 'em, an' they sure can give a feller an awful tossing". The boat didn't fare so well either: a few hours later it worked its way free of the moorings, shot over the lower steps of the falls, smashed to pieces and vanished.

The next year Faussett announced he would ride the twelve-metre-high Oregon City Falls in a new nine-metre boat which he believed was 'the finest craft on the water'. Things never went to plan with Faussett but this time they went more than usually haywire. A strong wind and current spun the boat around sideways at the edge of the rapids just as he was about to duck inside and shut the hatch for the jump. It turned over, twice perhaps, before he'd had time to shut the trapdoor, so he just hung on to the underside of the boat, breathing the air trapped in the space. "Going through those rapids sounded like a million cowbells to me". Faussett told *The Oregonian*. "You can't imagine the queer sensation of it". It took the rescue team six minutes to reach the upturned boat below the falls, but Faussett stepped out of the righted craft unhurt and smiling.

Next came the Silver Creek Falls, fifty-seven metres high. When nearby property owners refused to give Faussett the go-ahead, he simply bought the falls and forty hectares adjoining. Five thousand people watched Faussett drop over the falls in July 1928, in a round wooden contraption filled with thirty-six inner tubes from tyres and covered in orange canvas. Where the nose of this eighty-two-kg boat was meant to be wasn't clear, but wherever it was the boat failed to land on it, doing instead a tremendous belly-flop. Faussett, still protesting manfully about his lack of fear, broke a few ribs and a wrist and sprained both his ankles. In addition, his bowels seized up for four days.

Torn between ambition for himself and for his native area, Al Faussett dreamed of shooting the Niagara Falls but lit on the Shoshone Falls on Idaho's Snake River instead. He couldn't see a way of getting himself and the boat across country anyway. The Shoshone Falls may not be as well known as Niagara, but they are hardly small beer: at sixty-five metres they are fourteen metres higher than the famous tourist-puller. The canvas-covered ball of a boat was pressed into service again and a diversion dam was opened, by courtesy of the Idaho Power Company, to give him a bit more thrust. Even so, the boat twice got stuck on the bottom of the river and had to be manhauled over the edge.

Down dropped the boat, crack went the bones in Faussett's right hand, and up went the audience takings to $733.

Nobody has ever jumped a higher set of falls.

Until his death from cancer in 1948, Faussett continued to plan a ride over Niagara. He never made it but, as his son said, "He lived three lives to most men's one" and "got a lot of fun out of life".

All without learning to swim.

Pieces of Eight
In the USA there is a skydiving team that includes one world champion and a couple of other well-known figures in the sport. All eight jumpers are amputees and they call themselves Pieces of Eight.

The Truth at Last
Australian explorers have a jingle to explain why people go on expeditions:
   'It isn't for faith, fame or riches,
   Political favours or wealth,
   But to further the ends of some of his friends
   Who told him to ** himself.'

HANDSOME IS AS HANS DOES

Big Hans Tholstrup comes from one of Denmark's wealthiest families, a clan of long-lived, self-made people whose business interests range from liquid petroleum to the shipping of blue vein cheese. Hans' grandfather perfected Danish blue in 1959, when he was only 77. A fervent believer in capitalism and the rights of the individual, Tholstrup left home alone at the age of seventeen to travel the world. He ended up in Australia where "the country adopted me". The 90-kg bachelor with the bristling moustache and brusque manner runs several businesses in Sydney – cheese manufacture and expedition equipment retail among them. Money has helped him achieve his objectives but he has no time for professional sport, leaning to those pursuits in which everyone has an equal chance of success. After his early days in Australia, when he worked as a 'jackaroo' in the Northern Territory, shooting buffalo and driving road trains and bulldozers, he came to Sydney and for four years nursed a passion for motor racing. But he drifted out of that, explaining: "Life's too short to be fanatical about anything. You must experience as much as you can".

Now in his late thirties, Tholstrup has made it his business to do what 'can't be done'. Nearly always, he travels alone, maintaining that an individual's commitment is stronger than that of a group: a lone adventurer has only himself to blame if something goes wrong, but he is less likely to give up in the face of difficulties. Tholstrup spends a lot of his time in and around vehicles and indeed has been said to have power over inanimate objects, a gift he denies; nevertheless, his machinery rarely lets him down.

Among his adventures were what he called his 'Datsun dash' through Africa, a solo powerboat crossing of the Atlantic, a voyage around Australia alone in a five-metre outboard, and a singlehanded flight around the world, made just a week after earning his pilot's licence. In 1976, driving a tiny four-wheel-drive Daihatsu (958 cu. m FIOL), he repeated the route taken across Australia from its westernmost to its easternmost point by Mike and Mal Leyland ten years earlier. The Leyland brothers travelled in convoy; Tholstrup, of course, alone. He covered 5,800 km from Perth to Byron Bay, across the Gibson and Simpson Deserts, in just sixteen days. A sump guard, sand tyres, a winch and a bull-bar were added to the vehicle, but otherwise it was left as standard as possible. He drove fourteen or fifteen hours a day, averaging 35 kmph on the eleven-day transit proper. Highlights of the journey were the night in the Gibson Desert when the temperature fell to $-13C$, the lowest ever recorded there; the day he spent five hours digging the vehicle out of salt-pans; the tyre puncture caused by sharp spinifex grass growing, after recent rainfall, in the Simpson Desert; the 220-km detour he was forced to make to cross the swollen Eyre Creek; and the time the bull-bar collected a kangaroo.

In December 1982–January 1983, Tholstrup and his co-designer Larry Perkins crossed the continent again, from Perth to Sydney, in a small solar-powered car called *Solar Trek*. In an eighteen-day journey, they lopped ten days off their estimated crossing time, maintaining an average speed of 29 kmph. Sunlight was in plentiful supply in that antipodean summer, especially on the Nullarbor Plain, where temperatures easily passed the 40C mark. True to form, the civil servants in the New South Wales Department of Transport wanted to leave their imprint on the venture and insisted that the braking system in the car be replaced with a different kind before it could be allowed to cross the state to Sydney.

If Hans Tholstrup becomes the first person to drive up Mt. Fujiyama, to drive a Daihatsu from the southern-most tip of Tasmania to Cape York (floating across Bass

Strait on a barge), or to paddle a dugout canoe from New Guinea to Sydney, nobody will be in the least surprised – except perhaps Tholstrup himself, whose ambitions supersede each other faster than the average brain can follow.

LIFE JUMPS UP

'Ich lehre euch den Übermenschen. Der Mensch ist Etwas, das überwunden werden soll.'
(I teach you the superman. Man is something to be surpassed.)

– F.W. Nietzsche

'Just remember that every once in a while life jumps up and bites you in the ass: sometimes it feels good and sometimes it doesn't.'

– Jim Tyler

Jim Tyler used to treat death as small boys pester Mr Magoo. He'd go right up close, pull nasty faces, scatter a few well-placed banana skins, and run. Eventually Mr. Magoo got him.

Tyler was a criminal investigator with the U S Internal Revenue Service and the very antithesis of a bureaucrat. He'd horrify his colleagues by greeting his pay cheque with cries of "Ah, my monthly attendance allowance!". He was short, stocky, reasonably athletic, bright and very innovative; but of course he saved his most imaginative ideas for his leisure hours. When he died, he had about 1,600 parachute jumps to his credit. That's not a record, but his manner of achieving a few of that number takes some beating, not to say believing.

He specialised in stunt jumps of one kind and another. Sometimes he'd jump from weird places; or out of a plane and back in again; or he and his parachute would rendezvous in the sky. Here are some samples:

– Tyler and Bill Parsons, a cameraman and Tyler's 'lifeline', wearing jumpsuits, jumped from a plane about two or three seconds apart. To all intents and purposes, Tyler was parachuteless and convincingly feigned desperate mid-air contortions, for the benefit of television cameras, secure in the knowledge that he had a little emergency parachute inside the Velcro fastening of his jumpsuit. Taped to the arms of his suit were 'risers' – strips of webbing which connect a parachute harness to the suspension lines. Parsons had webbing taped to the inside back of his legs and connected to the middle of his harness. After jumping out, Tyler flew round to the back of Parsons and clipped the risers with two big butterfly-snaps into the D-rings on Parsons' leg webbing. Then Parsons deployed the parachute and both came down under the same canopy. Approaching the ground, Tyler jettisoned the first set of risers and connected to a six-metre set of lines. He was then able to drop the full six metres below his partner and become the first to land.

– For another television special, Tyler went up in a Steerman, an old military training bi-plane with fabric wings. As he jumped out, the Steerman dived. The plane had a parachute attached to it to keep it to a constant speed of 200 kmph. For Tyler it was a straightforward matter to grab the handles on the rear cockpit as the Steerman appeared beneath him, and to climb back in.

– On another occasion, Tyler threw a 40-quart (about 54 litres) mixing-bowl, with a parachute stretched across its mouth, out of a plane and jumped out after it. As the bowl, subject to variations in air pressure, danced crazily about the sky, Tyler, in freefall, seized the parachute, donned it, and came down under its canopy.

– The bridge of the *Queen Mary*, which is moored at Long Beach, California, is about twenty-seven metres above the water. Tyler's experiments with a particular parachute had shown it to open in about fifteen metres. Satisfied with this safety margin, Tyler decided to have a go at the *Queen*. He was almost stopped by a lady tour guide whose eye was caught as he climbed over a retaining wall. "Sir! ... Sir?" she called, half-scolding, half-questioning, "you're not authorised there!...?". But Tyler coolly assured her he'd be "through in a few minutes" and continued on up to the bridge, where he clipped a static line (an automatic deployment device) to a pole and jumped. Behaving more maliciously than in the test jumps, the parachute took its time opening, eventually coming into service after a fall of twenty-four metres – just three metres short of the water.

Said the guide, slightly peeved: "You know, they just never tell us when these special events are happening".

– Jim Tyler made about thirty-five 'fixed object' jumps – from cliffs, bridges and buildings. El Capitan in the Yosemite is a popular jumping-off point, but Tyler was one of only a couple of parachutists who jumped from a plane onto the summit, repacked his parachute, jumped again and landed at the foot of the cliff.

– Once, while ascending a stairwell to get to the roof of a building in Los Angeles, preparatory to a jump, Tyler and colleagues were alarmed to hear voices. Fearing they were about to be discovered, but being unable to pinpoint the direction from which the sound came, they dashed out onto one of the floors to hide. As luck would have it, the workmen stepped out onto the same floor. Tyler nipped behind a round pillar to avoid being seen, and remained there, dodging this way and that, as the workmen's line of vision changed, for an hour, like Buster Keaton on an off day. By the time it was safe to scarper off, the parachutists weren't afraid of jumping any more. "All the scare" they said "had already been scared out of us!"

– Then there was a jump from a 137-metre-high bridge in the San Diego area or, more accurately, from a dinky platform built on the back of a pickup truck. The truck was driven at 110 kmph across the bridge, close enough to the edge for the platform to protrude, and Tyler stepped off, over the deepest part of the canyon. As he did so, his foot slipped and he twisted and turned in flight. He managed to readjust his position and deploy his parachute, but not without a few exciting moments.

The excitement came to an end in Yosemite, on Half Dome, with its 600-metre vertical face and below that an extremely steep talus slope almost as high again. Line twists made Tyler's canopy uncontrollable and the parachutist was hammered against the wall two or three times. Tyler was observed fighting, but hit the ground already almost dead from head injuries.

Jimmy Tyler would never have done anything as restful as 'pass away'. Perhaps, having glimpsed the possibilities of superman, he could be said to have surpassed away.

Two-Faced Lady
'Adventure, someone has said, is a medal with two faces. On one, the goddess is seen winged, her suitcase by her side, ready for flights to parts unknown. On the other face she is seated at home mending socks.'

– Gertrude Baskine,
Hitch-Hiking the Alaska Highway.

NO BRIDGE TOO FAR

Per Arne Jeremiassen, a Norwegian adventurer in his early thirties, will do almost anything. Ask him why he likes to throw himself from antennae or drift around in a rubber boat and he retorts cheerfully "Why not?".

Most of his ideas come from friends and backers, and from combing newspapers and magazines to see what other people are doing – or, more to the point, *not* doing. He and his recently-formed company Adventure Enterprises are, however, open to suggestion and even to contract. Their slogan might be *Adventure for hire*. If you want someone to stand on a bar stool while a fast car is driven at it (and are prepared to pay to see it happen), Jeremiassen is your stool pigeon.

Long ago, when he was only an amateur loony, red-bearded, blue-eyed Jeremiassen used to be a deep-sea diver, with his own company. A lengthy illness proved the thinness of that cliché 'nobody's indispensable': since it was Jeremiassen individually who held all the relevant licences, the company was forced to go into liquidation (is that any place for an underwater outfit?). Afterwards, he worked for a while on the staff of an Oslo magazine, for which he now freelances. Jeremiassen doesn't just sit around and wait for news, however: he goes out and makes it.

It's perhaps not surprising that, in a country rich in mountains and coastline, Jeremiassen should focus on these features. But . . . cliff-jumping and bathtub-racing?

In 1980 Jeremiassen became the ninth person to parachute off the Trollveggen, a 400-metre sheer cliff in the Andalsnes region of Norway. (He would have been among the first if he hadn't been otherwise engaged a few weeks earlier.) He freefell for 200 metres, deployed the canopy and then, using a kind of steering device, 'flew' for 1,500–1,600 metres horizontally before landing. The Gerangefjord, where there is a sheer face 500–600 metres high, was the site of his second big cliff-jump. Here he landed in a rubber dinghy that was bobbing around in the waters of the fjord. He hit the headlines when he became the first person to jump from the 190-metre Europabrücke, the bridge over Austria's Brenner Pass, landing in a football field next to an electricity power station. Subsequent attempts by others to repeat the performance have been blocked by the authorities because of the danger that the short cuts from above may produce short circuits down below. Jeremiassen is associated with the American club BASE (for 'bridges, antennae, spans, earth'); membership is attained through fixed-object jumps. It is his contention that jumps can be safely performed from a height of as little as 100 metres (and it's been done, e.g. by Jim Tyler – see *Life Jumps Up*). Jeremiassen leads a lobby to legalise the 'sport' of fixed-object jumping in Norway, where his cautious compatriots continue to frown on it.

Meanwhile, he has several jumps and stunts up his sleeve. He'd like to drive a motorcycle off a cliff and at the last moment parachute free. (Pity the poor motorbike.) He aims to jump from a skilift – and tried it once, but was foiled when too many ordinary skiers got in the way. And there's a scheme to float through the air towed at the end of a 14-metre rope by a low-flying plane, before releasing to freefall and/or parachute to the ground.

Jeremiassen has also done a lot of dabbling in water sports. In 1981 he took part in a bathtub race, organised by a magazine, across a Norwegian fjord from the coast to an outlying island. To make things more interesting, he deliberately sabotaged his own entry, jettisoned his tub and climbed up on top of a kind of buoy – a balloon-shaped object atop a pole – waiting to be 'rescued'. Unfortunately, nobody noticed his absence. After six and a half hours, he resorted to swimming and was in the water for a further hour and a half before getting to within about 800 metres of the shore, when he was at last spotted and hauled in.

The following year, in an inflatable rescue dinghy with a 55 h.p. outboard motor – of the type used just offshore by the younger and fitter members of the RNLI – he tried twice to cross the English Channel and the

North Sea. The first time he followed a ferry out of Kristiansand but couldn't keep up with it. Then his compass broke and he lost his petrol tank, which left him without enough fuel to get to Britain. After drifting for twenty-two hours, he was only another six hours out of Newcastle when a Russian cargo boat, bound for France, happened by. The Russians insisted on altering course and taking the beleaguered Norwegian in to Newcastle, thereby perhaps helping international harmony more than the lone sailor, who would have been quite happy to be left on his own. Later in the summer, intending to wash up in Bergen in time for its 'French Week', he started from Paris in the same dinghy and motored down the Seine. As he crossed the Channel the keel split, and off the East Kent coast the boat broke up completely. After repairs he struggled on through the inland waterways but got no further than Birmingham. With Jeremiassen, one may always be sure of a next time, though.

Back on land, the 190-cm, 78-kg bachelor holds the world record for being thrown further than anyone else by another human being. A bouncer in an Oslo restaurant managed to toss our little friend a distance of 1.9 metres.

Jeremiassen also has his eye on the world speed roller-skating record, which currently stands at 240 kmph. Jeremiassen hopes to top 250 kmph by being towed by a Formula 1 or 2 racing car, and now needs only a venue – a 1,500–1,800-metre strait with a curved approach – to complete the necessary conditions.

One could devise a scenario in which Per Arne Jeremiassen is towed through the air by a plane and landed on a bridge, freefalls and parachutes from there into a motorised dinghy, 'sails' to a seaside restaurant, is thrown out by a bouncer onto a pair of roller-skates attached to a racing car and is whisked away, on a bar stool-strewn obstacle course, into the sunset. But one must steer clear of suggesting any such thing to Jeremiassen – because he'll only go and do it.

Heights of Enjoyment

Around Christmas-New Year 1981–2, four young men from Britain, one a qualified doctor, went to the Everest region on a trekking holiday. Twelve months of wishing, negotiating and letter-writing had hardened into a plan suitable for keen but inexperienced walkers. The trip involved hiring Sherpas and equipment, trekking from Chatara in the Terai northwards through an area hardly known to Europeans, crossing the Salpa Pass (4,000 metres) and two other passes over 3,000 metres, and at last reaching the summit of Kala Pattar (5,640 m). There the climbers were rewarded with marvellous views of Everest and its neighbour Nuptse, "surely', as the trip organiser Philip Judson wrote, "the most beautiful mountain in the world".

A praiseworthy trip, but why noteworthy? Because all four trekkers were members of the Cambridge-based Gay Outdoor Club, "originally set up at least in part to knock the popular idea that gay men were only interested in embroidery and Wagner.'

FIRE IN THE SNOW

John Waterman doesn't really fit into this book. But then, as his friends agreed, he didn't fit in anywhere. He was, they said, 'strong, determined, obsessed, insane'. He was also patently eccentric, a loner, a faddist and a dreamer. What he certainly was *not* was merely loopy; and his story is not funny but stunning and sad.

He was born in Washington, D.C., in September 1952, and disappeared in April 1981 while attempting a solo climb of the east buttress of Mt. McKinley. Into that short life he crammed a variety and intensity of experience that inundates the imagination and beggars belief. He began early. At the age of eleven he went with his father and a cousin on his first sustained hiking trip. In 1966, when he was 13, again with his father, he climbed all forty-six of the 4,000-footers in New Hampshire (the mountains over 1,220 metres) in one two-week trip. When he was fourteen, he decided to devote himself to mastering all aspects of mountaincraft. With a methodical thoroughness that bordered on mania, he practised, climbed, trained and exercised in all fields and all conditions. Much of this rigorous self-invention he undertook alone. After finishing school he went to Yosemite, the Canadian Rockies, England, Scotland, the Alps and Turkey, accounting for a large number of difficult ascents and routes. By 1972 the big mountains of Alaska had become the main focus of his interest. While working as a labourer on the Alaska pipeline, he would sneak off to explore new routes and climbs. In 1972 he made a first ascent of the east ridge of Mt. Huntington and in 1973, with three others, the first ascent of the south face of Mt. Hunter. In a race with an approaching storm, the team on that occasion mistook the south peak for the northern peak, and thus a prominent snow formation for the southern peak. They therefore stopped just sixty-five metres short of the 4,260-metre south summit. Although all the technical difficulties had been surmounted, they – in particular Waterman – felt they had unfinished business with the mountain.

It is for a later fierce engagement with Mt. Hunter that John Waterman will be best remembered. Hunter is the third highest peak in the Alaskan Range, after McKinley and Foraker, at 4,445 metres (the north summit) a beautiful, difficult mountain, far less often attempted than McKinley. More and more, Waterman had become preoccupied with solo climbing. He was attracted by Hunter's gigantic southeast spur, a spectacular 1,800-metre ridge which rises to join the south face from a point lower on the glacier. The spur, now recognised as one of the most elegant lines in the Alaskan mountains, had turned back two parties on previous attempts. Mt. Hunter had never been soloed before, by any route. By 1977, Waterman's ideas had fallen into place. He embarked on elaborate planning and preparations for a solo ascent of the southeast spur, followed by a traverse of the peak's summit plateau and a descent by the north side. When, in 1980, a team of three strong climbers repeated Waterman's route on the southeast spur, one of them reported it to be "without question the most aesthetic and difficult route on the mountain to date . . . destined to become a classic alpine style climb because of its appealing . . . beauty, lack of any easy climbing and the varied nature of the difficulties". "Waterman's Hunter climb defies being put in perspective", wrote Bradley Snyder, in Waterman's obituary in the *American Alpine Journal* 1982, ". . . while other superior climbers were concentrating on ever faster and lighter styles, John devoted an incredible 145 days to one of the slowest and heaviest climbs in history".

145 days! Waterman was flown in to the base of the mountain on 24th March 1978. Between then and 17th August he received by way of airdrops food and huge quantities of gear. The last flight to deliver supplies and collect superfluous equipment was on 19th April. The climber now had 1,100 metres of rope and seventy-four 5,000-calorie-per-day units of food, 360 kg in all. On that day Waterman said goodbye to the last human being he would see for more than three months.

The procedure Waterman had to adopt to ferry his supplies up the mountain was laborious in the extreme. He would climb a stretch, secure a rope to an anchor and descend, carry his equipment up the rope, return to retrieve the ropes and move on. He took an average of twelve round trips on each section of the ascent to shuttle his gear forward, and worked his way through about ten camps. In between, he had continuous difficult climbing to perform. The terrain throughout was exceedingly steep and technical; ice pinnacles popped up to block his path, backed up by sheer cliffs, blank walls, and long ice ridges with snow crests called cornices – traps for the unwary, since they have no support from below. Sometimes it took him an entire day to move twenty-five metres; other days he made no progress whatever, and in stormy weather and high winds he was forced to wait in his tent. Then, too, he would have the long and tedious job of shovelling snow off the roof to keep the weight from bending or breaking the poles.

In this time, he ran the gamut of human emotions, mostly from zero downwards. He lost a contact lens and suffered frostbitten fingers. At one point, he slipped while transferring his ice-axe to a higher position. As he had both hands on its shaft, he had no means of stopping his fall. What held him was a shoulder strap attached to his ice-hammer, which he had stuck in the slope just to get it out of the way and which, luckily, had been in solidly enough to support him. "The slip made me nervous", he recalled, with fine understatement. "It could have been fatal". On the summit plateau he had to climb on reduced rations to reach the airdrop site, which he reached just as his food ran out. Afterwards, he freely admitted to crying and screaming at the wind that kept the pilot from him. On 20th July, despite hurricane-force winds, the pilot flew in and dropped extra rations.

Meanwhile, Waterman had reached the south summit, leaning forward to kiss the buttress that topped the peak. With his additional food, but still carrying 270 kg of gear, he could now cross a three-km-wide plateau and climb another 460 metres to reach the north and highest summit, on 26th July. Three days later he saw people again – the first he had seen close up for a hundred days. Nineteen days later, he reached the bottom of the north side and flew out.

He had spent a scarcely credible time on an extreme route, on a major mountain, continuously exposed, entirely alone.

The climb changed him. Some of the old idiosyncracies remained: he still darted around in dramatic clothes, wore blue glasses with a star between the lenses, smoked the odd joint, made music, occasionally threw temper tantrums, was consistently unpredictable, and proclaimed the benefits of his protein-free diet. But the mountains and the elements had become still more real to him, and more challenging. They, more than his fellow humans, had become his companions, and he invested them with the frailties and duplicities, the enticements and charms of real people, relating to them powerfully and responding only to them with his true essence.

From here it was almost a foregone conclusion that he should go on to the ultimate adventure – a solo traverse of Alaska from tidewater to tidewater, south to north, on foot, crossing over Mt. McKinley – which exacted from him the ultimate price. John Waterman was, like the character described by Jack Kerouac in *On the Road*, one of the "mad ones, the ones who are mad to live, mad to talk, mad to be saved, desirous of everything at the same time, the ones who never yawn or say a commonplace thing, but burn, burn, burn . . ."

Only the snow could put out such a flame.

GOING TO EXTREMES

'In my youth,' Father William replied to his son,
'I feared it might injure the brain;
But now that I'm perfectly sure I have none,
Why, I do it again and again!'
– Lewis Carroll, Alice in Wonderland.

GOING ROUND THE WORLD MAKES THE WORLD GO ROUND

The story so far: Once upon a time there lived a young-at-heart man who occupied a medium-sized house on the edge of a big city called London. He had a great fortune (a six-figure salary earned by building up his own reinsurance company from nothing to a value of over £20 million in seventeen years), he was clever (though at school he had compared unfavourably with Simple Simon) and he was blessed with good health (distributed equably throughout a generous volume of flesh). He loved to wander (travelling nearly 500,000 km a year on business, mostly by Concorde), enjoyed playing games (VDU terminals, telexes, word processors and other computers), spent cosy evenings chopping wood (to build record-sized bonfires of twenty metres or more – one of his more bizarre hobbies) and often went to market (where he bought 100 tons of railway sleeper, from British Rail, for use in constructing the above bonfires). He had many friends (famous cartoonists, influential journalists and fellow businessmen, who elected him Salesman of the Year 1981). But he was lonely and sad, for want of a good wife.

NOW READ ON . . .

Sitting next to David Springbett on a flight from Caracas to London one day in the late 1970s was an attractive twenty-five-year-old girl. They got talking; Springbett got interested. Had the young lady – Paddy by name and a former air stewardess – ever been married, Springbett wondered. No. Never considered it? Well, there had been this Austrian called Arnold. He, she explained, had been personable and pleasant and a stunning-looking man with a magnificent physique, but she hadn't wanted a husband who did what Arnold did for a living. Later that evening, after a promising dinner for two, Arnold's name popped up again. If only you could lose a little weight, Paddy was hinting, you too could have a beautiful body like Arnold's. Oh yes, she said again, she would have married Arnold if it hadn't been for what he *did*. Springbett, whose senses were by now aroused in more ways than one, could suddenly contain his curiosity no longer. What *was* it exactly that Arnold, this Adonis, did? Oh, didn't I tell you? asked Paddy. Arnold's surname was Schwarzenegger. He was Mr. Universe; his colour photo adorned a quarter page of the *Guinness Book of Records.*

David Springbett's motor instantly took a U-turn. Taking in the 'detour' sign, he cast a quick glance at the romantic map and spotted the best alternative route to getting his girl. Obviously, he figured, *he* would have to set a world record and get his photo in the record books. But which record? Fare-paying travel on scheduled airlines was a clear candidate, and a look at the existing records convinced him that he could do better.

So it was that in 1980 he set off from Los Angeles round the world. Travelling at an average speed of 1,064 kmph, he became the fastest man ever 'within the atmosphere'. He left Los Angeles in a British Airways Boeing 747 at 7 pm one Tuesday (3 am Wednesday London time) and flew to London, where he boarded a

Concorde for Singapore, via Bahrain. From Singapore he flew to Bangkok, Manila, Tokyo and Honolulu, arriving back in Los Angeles aboard a United Airlines 747, just 44 hours and six minutes after he had left. He flew a total of 37,124 km, 336 km more than the length of the Tropic of Cancer, the distance required for a round-the-world record.

With this flight he beat the previous record of 53 hours, 34 minutes for scheduled air passengers, set in 1978 by three Australian journalists, and a world record for an air circumnavigation set by the crew of a US Air Force B-52 bomber. Even with a refuelling in the air, the American plane could only manage a tortoise-like 45 hours, 19 minutes.

Springbett, who believes there is no such thing as jet lag, flew straight back to London afterwards, still fresh despite having had only two hours' sleep in the previous sixty-eight hours and having eaten nothing but airline food for two days. The worst mishap of the whole venture was when his tie fell down a lavatory pan.

Ever the wheeler-dealer, Springbett had ensured that the record-smashing trip would not cost him a penny. By betting $500 at 20–1 that he could beat the record, he raised enough money to cover his fare of $8,000 and expenses.

The 1981 edition of the *Guinness Book of Records* carried an item on the new record and a quarter page colour photo of the holder.

In February 1982, Springbett set two new world records, for the fastest transatlantic flights in both directions between London (Trig Lane Helipad by St. Paul's Cathedral) and New York (Wall Street Heliport). A communication chain of fifty-eight links included radio connections between helicopter and Concorde, the closure of Heathrow airport to all other traffic for two minutes around the time of take-off, and clearance for the helicopter to land on the main Jumbo runway, within twenty metres of the Concorde. At the urging of the helicopter company, the record attempts were made in February, when weather conditions – especially on the eastbound flight – were less than ideal. Even so, David Springbett achieved the crossings in three hours, 59 minutes, 44 seconds (westbound) and three hours, 40 minutes, 40 seconds (eastbound), cutting about eleven minutes off existing records.

Now that he's riding firmly on a bandwaggon of his own creation, David Springbett would dearly like to become the record-holder of record-holders. If he could slip *three* records into the *Guinness* book – preferably in different categories, land, sea and air – he would have more entries to his name than any other holder. The Beatles rate a mere two. With the permission of the police and local authorities, he may yet get to build his mooted hundred-metre bonfire. And with the kind consent of his bank to an overdraft of £1 million (not yet forthcoming), he would like to regain for Britain the Blue Ribbon Trophy for the fastest transatlantic crossing by a passenger-carrying vessel. Springbett, as the statutory passenger, would ride in a purpose-built twenty-metre boat piloted by a speedboat champion, the 1,865 kw gas turbine helicopter engine being refuelled four times en route by RAF Hercules planes. The record has been held by the *United States* since her maiden voyage in 1952.

And, speaking of maidens . . . what has all this highly charged activity done for David Springbett? Although the pace of his life has stepped up a notch, he hasn't changed much, except that he isn't lonely any more. In fact, he seems set fair to live happily ever after. And his wife – that is, Mrs. Paddy Springbett, former air stewardess, now mother of two – thinks so too.

> **Overkill Over The Arctic**
> Count Guido Monzino is an Italian millionaire and
> professional explorer, not necessarily in that order.
> In 1958 he led a team to make the first assault on
> the Paine group in Patagonia, reaching the summit
> of the Paine Grande, and in 1973 he riled dedicated
> mountaineers everywhere by launching an ascent
> of Everest from a comfortably carpeted base camp
> to which he had been flown in by helicopter. That
> expedition numbered sixty-four climbers, chosen
> from Italian mountain troops, and about a thousand
> Sherpas. In between, in 1970, he had got to the
> North Pole with the daily help of a spotter aircraft
> and a Hercules C-130 transport plane, 150 dogs,
> half a dozen Eskimos and five others. Money can't
> buy love, even among expeditioners, and there was
> much dissent and disappointment along the way.
> Asked if he would make the journey again, he
> replied vigorously in the negative: "Too much, too
> much of everything. Too much danger. Too much
> cold." After the expedition, at great cost, he flew
> his dogs back from the Arctic, even though they
> would never be used again and were not wanted
> by anyone else. "Beautiful dogs", he explained. 'Very
> fast.'

DEADLY ENEMIES

As a young man of 22, John Fairfax fell in love. When
the affair finished he was sorry for a time, but as years
went by and optimism began again to shine through he
began to be glad about it. It meant, he said, that he was
indestructible.

Emotionally indestructible he may be. But however strong the spirit is, all human flesh is much the same – vulnerable – and his has suffered enough ravages to make him realise that even a survivor doesn't survive for ever. In his case, the end is likely to come swiftly.

"I'll probably come a cropper with a shark one day."

John Fairfax, you will remember, is the man who rowed the Atlantic alone and later rowed the Pacific with his companion Sylvia Cook. One way and another, sharks have loomed large in his adventures.

On the Atlantic, he fought a hammerhead, keeping the head as a trophy, discarding the fins and feeding the rest to the dorados which accompanied his boat – he called them 'my boys'.

On the 32nd day out, while he was scraping barnacles off the hull, he sensed and then saw an immense mako shark gliding towards him. There was no time for him to try for the safety of the boat. Fairfax decided on defence by attack. He lunged with his knife, caught the beast in the underbelly and, as the shark thrust itself away, ripped it open from mouth to tail.

Later, on a day when he was ill with a fever and vomiting over the side, he saw a tiger shark 'looking very mean' circling his boat. As he stared at it, "an overpowering hate slowly began to boil up inside me and suddenly, screaming like a madman, I pulled out my knife and dived at it". This one was, fortunately, in no mood for a fight to the death. They skirmished for a while, until the shark at last wearied of the irritation and disappeared.

In an attempt to raise £10,000 to finance his second grand design, Fairfax offered to fight any shark – other than a great white. No newspaper took up the challenge. Shark Fight Idea Number Two was then put into operation: Fairfax would fight the shark on camera and sell the resulting film. Off the Bahamas, he fought and did indeed kill a 2.5-metre hammerhead. The film proved the facts but its second class quality made it unsaleable. A second attempt also failed to produce good film. The *Sunday People* bought the story and paid him enough to cover his expenses, but there was little enough left over for the row itself. At that point, Fairfax, who had contracted to write the account of his Atlantic voyage, "ran out of brilliant ideas and sat down to finish the book".

Be that as it may, this was not to be Fairfax's last encounter with a shark. In March 1972, Fairfax, in mid-Pacific with Sylvia Cook, was over the side, fishing. A small white tip shark, idling by, took it into its head to nose in on his catch. This brazenness was too much for Fairfax, who speared it through the head. The spear stuck and Fairfax struggled to retrieve it, at last pulling it free. This should have been the end of the incident, but it wasn't.

"Problem is, I hate sharks so much I just couldn't resist the temptation of doing a real job on that one."

So, with a buck knife passed to him by Sylvia, he ripped the shark's belly open. Fairfax held fast to the writhing creature until its flailing weakened and he knew that it was approaching its end. Then he relaxed his grip. But there was life in the shark yet. With a last great burst of energy, it streaked up behind Fairfax and clamped its teeth into his upper right arm. He tore the shark away and in doing so gave the dying creature its last meal – a huge chunk of his own flesh.

The wound he suffered was fifteen cm long, three cm wide and three cm deep – "ghastly", as Sylvia wrote, looking "like a joint of veal, pulsating and bleeding profusely".

The arm healed. John Fairfax lives to fight again. But who knows what will happen when next the deadly enemies meet?

I'M GRINGO. FLY ME

Classical place names are rare in Australia. Settlers tend to have chosen names that reminded them of home, not of Homer. The best-known exception is the Nullarbor Plain, so called because no tree grows there. The Nullarbor's bleakness isn't just a matter of there being no trees. It's a semi-desert of dirt, bull-dust and rock. Not the sort of place which anyone with sense would try to traverse on a motorcycle.

Volker Lenzner did: though it might be more accurate to say that he flew – if only a few centimetres above the ground. He experimented with slow speeds, but all that happened was that he flopped in and out of the desert's deep corrugations like a rag doll. This was no place for pussyfooting. Gritting his teeth, he urged his motorbike *Gringo* to 70 or 80 kmph and charged at the sand-swollen highway, sheer velocity causing him to skim the furrows and swells. He became a pilot navigating his jet just clear of the desert surface, looking out all the while for the best skid, preparing every instant for an emergency landing.

Two minutes, five minutes, twenty minutes went by and all was well. In a state of electrified alertness, Lenzner whizzed past six or seven cars, hurling dirt into the eyes of drivers, whose startled expressions forecast disaster. For 430 km he hurtled along, wondering how long his luck would hold out.

Not long. As darkness fell, Lenzner hit a huge pothole at 60 kmph. *Gringo* moaned, trembled and lunged into the air. For three seconds, machine and rider cavorted in the air; then, acrobatics over, they headed for earth, slamming full tilt into the ground, spinning and skidding before eventually grinding to a halt. *Gringo* rattled pitifully and was silent. Beaten and soiled, she lay with her handle folded in, her cables and saddle bags ripped off.

157

Lenzner camouflaged the bike near the crash site and hitched a lift into Ceduna, 44 km down the road, where a panelbeater was engaged to collect and repair the grounded BMW jet-bike. Lenzner himself was less easy to restore to his former health and beauty, having left several layers of skin from his rear, legs, fingers and torso at the crash site, with only bumps and bruises added to make up for the loss.

Instead of taking the hint fate had dropped, Lenzner heaved himself back in the saddle and proceeded to traverse the rest of the continent.

Later, in Queensland, Lenzner was heading west from Townsville along the Flinders Highway. Cowboy country, where the road conditions deteriorate and signposting dwindles to nothing, causing a driver to halt time and again to check the route.

One missing signpost and another pointing to nowhere alerted Lenzner's long-dormant instinct for caution – but it was overridden, as were also 130 km of sand. Now he realised that the town shown on the map wasn't there. Worse, he discovered with horror a yawning emptiness in *Gringo*'s petrol tank. Out of fuel, on the wrong track, in no-man's-land. The nearest petrol station was 200 km back.

Gradually, another fact seeped through into Lenzner's brain. Those ruts in the dirt were ancient. No recent traveller had passed this way. "You are stuck", he told himself. "Now you will rot."

Boy Scout dogma and survival instinct prevailed, however, and after a quick calculation, which revealed that four and a half litres of drinking water plus some canned food and biscuits would last a week, he settled down in his sleeping bag to wait.

And even dropped off to sleep, until a sudden commotion interrupted his dreams in the small hours of the morning. A car! A second later, Lenzner, his eyes dazzled by two glaring headlights, was up, waving frantically and shouting, like a castaway signalling to a passing ship.

"Damn lucky, you are", said the driver in a voice that was music to Lenzner's ear. He had taken a short cut; only a few cars ever came that way. Little things mean a lot. Along with nine litres of petrol bought from the motorist, Volker Lenzner also purchased the chance to remain in the land of the living. His sole thought then was to head back towards the junction of the Flinders Highway and boom and burn away from it as fast as his little wheels could carry him.

Crossing the Line to Lunacy
Most good scientific expeditions raise more questions than they answer. Sometimes this is true of bad non-scientific expeditions as well.

The plan to have an all-female team 'swimming' the Atlantic in a heated swimming pool towed by a vessel, for example, raises lots of questions. Nobody has any answers, not even the originators. This is one brainchild that ought to be thrown out with the bathwater.

Antique Antics
In 1901 John Voss spent eighty silver dollars on the purchase of a dugout canoe named *Tilikum*. The vessel was then known to be a century old. In it, Voss nearly accomplished a circumnavigation of the globe. Nobody had attempted such a feat before, nor has it been repeated since. *Tilikum* is today the world's oldest surviving transocean 'yacht'.

HAIL THE CONQUERING ANTI-HERO

Waseca, Minnesota, (population 6,700) is a place of no great distinction, and of no great dishonour either. The town and one of its inhabitants, David Kunst, tolerated each other well enough for some three decades. Married, with three small children, Kunst was head of a county survey crew and also worked by night as a projectionist at the local cinema. What remained of his spare time was given over to his passion: drag racing. Then suddenly 'something snapped'. He grew tired of his job, of Waseca, and of its 'lot of little people who didn't want to think'. Kunst denounced his 6,699 fellow-Wasecans as 'hypo-critical, petty, self-righteous and narrow-minded'. Then, wisely, he got out before they threw him out.

"I made up my mind that I would do something that would be a little different", Kunst stated. Actually, what he did was quite a lot different, as the record books attest. Starting in June 1970 and continuing until October 1974, Kunst achieved the first ever verified 'walk around the world'. Using aeroplanes to carry him across water, he nevertheless trudged 24,000 km through thirteen countries before wheeling back into his home town and the welcome of 5,000 forgiving Wasecans.

Initially, he was accompanied by his younger brother John and a mule donated by the Waseca Chamber of Commerce, thereby attracting the dismissive label 'two asses and a mule'. They weren't particularly fit or attuned to walking and the older Kunst's wife Jan "kept expecting him to call and say 'Come over and pick us up' ". Gradually, however, they got into their stride, toughened up and picked up a few tricks of the road, until they were averaging 65 km a day. Gifts of cough drops and army rations came their way, as did royal greetings (from the late Princess Grace of Monaco among others) and offers of accommodation. In Manhattan the Kunsts assumed that the invitation to stay at a Holiday Inn extended to the mule and were dismayed to find that their four-legged friend's presence indoors was unwelcome – the more so when the animal relieved himself in the hotel lobby before he could be led off and tethered. In Iran and Turkey, the pair were stoned by locals hostile to Americans; in France and Spain they were mistaken for smugglers and criminals.

Much worse was to come. In 1972, near Kabul, the pair were attacked by Afghan bandits who believed that their victims were carrying substantial sums of money collected for charity. (In fact, the Kunsts had been collecting only pledges for UNICEF, not cash, and had just a few dollars on them at the time.) John Kunst, then 25, was shot dead. David flew back to Waseca where he waited three months for a bullet hole in his lung to heal. Then, along with his other brother Peter, he resumed the journey where he had left off, walking to Calcutta and on to and through Australia. Permission to enter China was refused.

On his return, David Kunst, who admitted openly that he had frequently 'enjoyed female companionship' along the way, announced that he had no intention of resuming married life or of living in Waseca again. At the welcome-home ceremony, however, champagne or largesse prompted him to proclaim the U.S.A. 'the best damn country I've ever been in'. But 'being in' and settling down are not the same thing. "I'm a social deviate," he said, "a radical, even a little crazy. I don't fit into anybody's pattern and I never will".

BORN-AGAIN FLYER

Michael Bartlett loves flying and strives to impart his love of it with all the fervour and zeal of a missionary. This is precisely what he is. Written after his name is 'O.G.S.', which could stand for 'On God's Service' but doesn't. In fact, the little flock of letters marks him out as a member of the Anglican Oratory of the Good Shepherd, in Canterbury, Kent. He has worked in mission hospitals in Zululand and at Maseru in Lesotho. This gentleman is also contributing editor to the magazine *Business Traveller* and the only one of that breed, according to them, actually to enjoy sitting in aircraft cabins.

Michael Bartlett is, put bluntly, an air travel fanatic. In his first ten years of flying, from 1969 to 1979, he visited 86 airports in 45 countries and travelled with 52 airlines in 43 types of aircraft. His 208 flights lasted 284 hours and 22 minutes. He covered a total of 154,648 km and travelled on the last planned scheduled flights of the Bristol Wayfarer, the HS Comet 4 and the Aviation Traders Carvair (DC-4 conversion).

It hadn't taken him long to be converted. Within two years of the first revelation, he had notched up fifty flights and become an avid reader of airline literature, timetables, maps and schedules.

Not everyone found this sort of thing admirable. In Bucharest, for example, Bartlett arrived late one evening, owing to engine trouble on the incoming plane, and missed the connecting flight to Budapest. When he declined the offer of hotel accommodation, the traveller, after much discussion and translation under the scrutiny of an armed policeman, was escorted to the top of the airport building and locked in a comfortable room for the night – presumably for the simultaneous protection of passenger and national security. In the morning he was woken on time, given breakfast and escorted in style to the plane after the other passengers had boarded.

In Budapest, the problem of proselytising took a different turn. The lady at the airport information desk simply couldn't understand that Bartlett just wanted to fly around Europe, with different airlines and in different types of aircraft.

"But where do you want to go?" she kept asking.

"Anywhere", Bartlett kept replying.

In 1980, *Business Traveller* magazine took Braniff Airways up on its offer of two weeks' unlimited travel on its domestic networks for a fixed price of $349. They bought Michael Bartlett a first class Braniff Air Pass and sent him off to see how much mileage could be squeezed out of the deal. His target was at least 55 flights.

He reckoned, however, without computers and other unholy creations. Booked on a round trip to Albany, New York, from Newark, New Jersey, he volunteered to give up his seat on the outgoing flight as it was over-booked. With his permission, his luggage went on without him, to be returned on the same plane. Not having travelled to Albany, Bartlett naturally failed to present himself there for his flight back to Newark. The computer inwardly digested and spat out its reply: labelling him a 'no-show', it wiped his entire itinerary from its records. Dazzling with its feats of both electronic and mechanical trickery, the airline contrived also temporarily to misplace his luggage on the Albany-Newark route.

In the end, by shifting into overdrive, sprinting about between airport gates and collapsing with exhaustion whenever he had a free moment, Michael Bartlett brought his tally of flights in that highly charged fortnight to about fifty – with the help, perhaps, of the good Captain in the Sky.

Dead End

In the early 1960s Klaus Denart, of Hamburg, tried to 'sail' down the Blue Nile in a coffin. If this indicated some kind of death wish he was certainly disappointed, for he is today alive and well and running an expedition equipment shop in his home town.

Swimming Down Britain

Jill Russell, a librarian at Cambridge University and the mother of three children, suffers from a disabling rheumatic condition. To alleviate her own discomfort and to raise money for charity, she goes swimming in her local pool. Every day, after work, she plies back and forth, often as many as 325 lengths. In her sponsored swims, she has now done the equivalent of two complete lengths of Britain, travelling 'down' from John O'Groats to the Isle of Wight (first time) or Land's End (second). She says she finds it psychologically easier to imagine herself swimming from north to south, since anyone looking at a map knows that that is 'downhill'!

CATALOGUES OF DISASTER

But oh, beamish nephew, beware of the day,
If your Snark be a Boojum! For then
You will softly and suddenly vanish away,
And never be met with again!
> – Lewis Carroll, *The Hunting of the Snark,*
> Fit 3. *The Baker's Tale.*

ARMCHAIR EXPLORER

Seeing the world by floating through the air in a comfortable chair is something most of us would consider the ideal method of exploration. It's a fantasy, of course, and quite impossible. Or is it?

Larry Walters, a 33-year-old truck driver from Long Beach, California, dreamed that dream for about three months, putting about $4,000 into buying equipment for an airborne seat. He planned to launch himself in a lawn chair, with the aid of forty-five helium-filled meteorological balloons, going up perhaps two thousand metres. A dozen or so friends stood by as he prepared for lift-off in July 1982. As they let go of the chair's ropes, the tether securing it to the ground broke, and up went Larry, shooting skywards like an elevator.

Too high for comfort, in fact. Within minutes he was sending out a Mayday call from his chair-mounted CB radio. A listener said: "This guy broke into our channel . . . He sounded worried, but he wasn't panicked". At 5,000 metres, the garden flying machine attracted the attention of pilots of common flying machines, who eyed Larry with some incredulity and concern. Also,

Larry began to feel a little chilly. With an airgun he had taken with him, he shot at several of the balloons and so began to descend. "The part that was scary was the last hundred metres, with the rooftops and telephone wires coming up so fast. I was praying that I wouldn't hit one of those power lines and be fried". The balloon ropes did become entangled in a power line, briefly blacking out a small area of Long Beach and leaving Larry dangling, uninjured, until rescuers could reach him.

He had been airborne for over an hour.

"It fulfilled my dream," said Larry afterwards, "but I wouldn't do this again for anything".

Nor will he be allowed to. Mr. Neal Savoy, a regional safety inspector of the US Federal Aviation Administration, took a dim view of the performance. "We know he broke some part of the law", he said. "As soon as we decide which part it is, some charge will be filed. If he had a pilot's licence, we'd suspend that, but he doesn't".

In future, Larry Walters may have to stick to conventional armchair exploration.

Tailpiece

In December 1982, the Federal Aviation Administration finished deliberating about which part of the law Walters had broken. Dangling in front of him the threat of a $4,000 (£2,500) fine, it concluded that he had been guilty of

– 'operating a civil aircraft for which there is not currently in effect an air-worthiness certificate',

– 'operating an aircraft without establishing and maintaining two-way communication with Long Beach control tower', and

– 'creating a traffic hazard'.

The lapse of five months simply made the FAA crosser about the incident, but Walters obviously felt a lot cheerier. He announced his intention both to challenge the proposed fines and to take another ride in his canvas and aluminium 'aircraft'.

166

"It's my sincere belief" he said "that if the FAA had been around when the Wright brothers were testing their aircraft, they would never have been able to get it off the ground".

Governments the world over seem to believe that the air belongs to them and not to the people. In the Eastern bloc, ordinary mortals require permission virtually to breathe it; in the West, only to float around in it.

A Czech on Progress
At home in Prague one day, jet engineer Milos Urban found himself reading an account of the 1908 Great Race sponsored by the *New York Times* and Paris' *Le Matin*. Inspired, he gathered together three like-minded friends – a television journalist, a glazier and a plumber – to make a similar epic journey. They acquired two vintage Czech-made and -registered cars – one a 1924 two-cylinder Tatra roadster – and planned an itinerary that was supposedly less ambitious than that of 1908 but nevertheless stretched from New York to Paris, taking in Alaska, the Bering Strait and the USSR.
The four young men went west, as far as central Alaska, crossing bridges only as they came to them. But then their hopes of reaching the Bering Strait were dashed when they reached the junction of the Yukon and Tanana Rivers, just west of Manley Hotsprings, and found no bridge to take them further . . .

HUNTER AND THE NIMROD VARIATION

"I can remember several instances in my life when I

have had to waste time and wait, but this had to beat the lot".

Geoffrey Hunter's experience also tops most stories anyone else could tell about waiting. His long wait took place one cold night while he was circumnavigating the coast of Britain – on top of a buoy in the Solway Firth.

The 3,200-km voyage, in an Eskimo kayak or angmagssalik, lasted from May to November 1970, with nightly stops for food, rest and repairs. His kayak was named *Nimrod*, after an earlier hunter.

One Friday at the end of July he struck out from Kippford on the Scottish side of the Solway Firth for Workington, in England. There was a mist and a heavy swell. Murky brown water seeped into the boat and slopped about in the cockpit. This went on for two hours, by which time Hunter was exactly halfway across and the boat was half full of water. Hunter tried vainly to bale it out with his hat. The boat lumbered and slewed about with the added weight. A row of chimneys momentarily drifted into view through a break in the mist, giving Hunter brief confirmation of his direction-finding. Navigating by compass bearing, he pressed on. In fact, he pressed so hard on the blade in order to try and still the rolling motion of the boat that it splintered and cracked in two. At the same moment the boat sank and overturned. Unable to right himself by means of the usual eskimo roll – because the hull was so low down in the water, and he was hampered by his life-jacket – Hunter saw that the only thing for it was to get out of the boat. Undoing the spray deck he surfaced. The boat now turned the right way up, though it still brimmed with water. Hunter collected all the loose floating pieces, strapped one half of the paddle under the elastic on the stern deck, scooped up the seat which had come adrift and put it back in the boat and locked it. Then he turned the boat back upside down and, gripping the other half-paddle to the side of the boat, did a backward roll in the cockpit, positioned the paddle and lurched himself back into an upright sitting position. He then had a moment to think but, as he noted laconically, "with just half a paddle it was two or three minutes before I gained confidence".

The boat continued to roll and pitch, the current kept on sweeping in and out of the Solway Firth and the mutilated paddle provided negligible leverage. Hunter had eight km to go before he reached Workington. He reckoned this would take him perhaps another twelve hours in his unmanoeuvrable boat, if he wasn't dragged out by the current into the Irish Sea in the meantime. He cast around for a way out and spotted in the distance a buoy, then the size of a dot. He headed towards it, thinking he would hook on to it and wait for help.

Fifty minutes' further toil brought him close to the buoy, but a swift current made it impossible for him to turn the boat in towards it. He undid the painter, tied it round his waist and leapt out of the cockpit. Swimming against the tide, he spent another three quarters of an hour towing *Nimrod* the last 40 metres to the buoy. At last he reached it, curled the painter round it and, resting on the boat, took a breather. Beginning to feel the cold with the cessation of his exertions, he blew his emergency whistle until his face was red and his ears almost hissing with steam. Nothing happened.

He decided to get up on the buoy, which was the shape of an upturned bucket, about 1.3 metres in diameter on the top, splaying out to about two metres at the bottom. The smooth slimy sides stood nearly two metres out of the water. Reasoning that there must be a hook on top, Geoffrey Hunter pushed the painter up so that it would catch on the hook. At the sixth attempt it locked on the top. Heaving up on the painter, Hunter brought *Nimrod* halfway up the buoy. After further intense struggle with the sea, the weight of the boat and of his own body the roughness of the cord and the slipperiness of the buoy, he used *Nimrod* as a step and heaved himself in a sitting position astride the buoy. The painter mooring the boat to the hook cut into Hunter's leg as the buoy rolled one way and *Nimrod* surfed along the wave in the opposite direction. If he could haul the whole boat out of the water, he thought, he could rest it across the buoy and then also reach his flares and food, stored in watertight compartments of the boat. Try as he might, he couldn't lift the boat and had to let her drift again.

After another half an hour the weight of the boat grew too much for the painter and it snapped.

Hunter sat solemnly watching *Nimrod* drift off with the tide and silently bidding goodbye to his supplies. He knew the boat wouldn't sink and would probably drift in with the tide. But going after it was out of the question.

By 9 pm dusk was falling and his "near joyful attitude at being in this exciting situation slowly sank to the depressing thought of never putting foot on dry land again".

Just to be on the safe side, he began swearing at the inefficiency of the Coastguard, who had been advised of his plans and should have been out looking for him. By ten o'clock he had resigned himself to spending the night on the buoy. He had two metres of the painter left where it had snapped and, winding it round himself twice and then back onto the hook, he put his arm through the hook, slung himself sideways and curled up into a ball.

Dozing and drifting, he swung round and round on his four fathom bank buoy, the clank of its taut chain on the metal his only diversion. Time and again he got stiff and shifted sides, swinging over the hook to lock his other arm through. Often he looked at his watch, but the time passed no faster for it.

At 5 am it began to get light, but the thick shroud of mist did not clear for another hour and a half. Now he could at least identify his goal. The tide was on the last of the ebb; by seven o'clock it would start the six hours of flood up into the Solway. If he had to swim for it, now would be the time, for he would be swept towards the land. Staying put until the afternoon would give the Coastguard and the Lifeboatmen more time to find him, but by then the tide would have turned. Later still, he would be so low on enthusiasm, food and sleep that he would not have the energy to make land.

About one and a half km away there was another buoy at the edge of a shipping channel. The buoy that had accommodated him marked a sand bank: larger vessels steered clear of it. Trusting in his lifejacket, he made his decision. At 7 am he let go of the hook and slipped into the water. The cold gave him a shock. Plodding mindlessly on through the water for some indeterminate time he reached the other buoy, which offered no holds at all along its towering striped sides. There was nothing for it but to swim on across the shipping lane and try to reach Workington. Hunter's progress was tedious and slow but steady. The whistle was pressed into service whenever a boat came near, but again and again boats passed by without responding to the call.

At last a very small dinghy came splashing through the water in his direction. Two couples dragged the swimmer into the already overloaded boat. He slumped in the bottom, shivering uncontrollably, limp with relief. His rescuers took him ashore and drove him to hospital. There he had a visit from the police who took a statement and told him that six lifeboats and two helicopters had been looking for him.

In order to continue his voyage, Hunter now needed another kayak. He nipped down to London and borrowed one from a friend. Adapted, this became *Nimrod II*.

A few days later *Nimrod* the First was found on a slag heap only 400 metres from the Coastguard's lookout.

The equipment under the hatches was intact but the boat itself was a write-off, most of the plywood having been pummelled on the rocks until it resembled papier mâché.

Was Geoffrey Hunter lucky or unlucky? Probably both. Paddling an Eskimo kayak around Britain is a risky business and things are liable to go wrong. *His* view was that he was "lucky to be only changing canoes, and not exchanging his earthly existence for the 'other place".'

Man and Fireman
During a 125-km foot safari between two base camps on the Tana River Expedition (1976), Christopher Portway happened to be on his own at night when he met a 'great tusker'. He charged at the animal, brandishing a flaming faggot from the remains of the camp fire. This, as Portway admitted a bit sheepishly afterwards, is 'not at all the way to treat wild elephants'. The beast beat a retreat nonetheless and all was well – except that Portway had to spend the next hour beating out the forest fire he'd started.

SPANISH BULL

In 1980, four Spaniards, professional men all, went on an expedition to the Andes Mountains. There they were struck with an idea: they would ride motorcycles to the North Pole!

Back in Spain, José Maria Molina, 32, and Antonio Axerio, 29, both chemists, Aurelio Rodriguez, 32, an engineer, and a 36-year-old doctor, Javier de Pablo, had four 350 c.c. motorcycles with a low gearing system built to their specifications by a company called Bultaco. The foursome had considered using dogs, snow scooters, cars and a balloon for the journey, but had come back to the idea that motorcycles were best. Four sledges were built to carry gear and petrol for the 4,000-km ride. In difficult conditions the motorcycles would move together in a fan shape with the sledges attached to each other in line. Clothing too was specially made for the expedition. The total cost of the venture was to be one million Norwegian kroner (about £87,000), of which the team members themselves contributed 60,000 Kr (over £5,000), the remainder being raised from sponsors.

None of the team had previous experience of polar regions, but they had great faith in their motorcycles and equipment, which performed satisfactorily during a week's tests on a frozen lake in the Pyrenees. They planned to travel to the east coast of Spitsbergen and then venture onto the ice.

Spitsbergen is not the ideal starting point for an expedition to the North Pole: the currents, ice movements and climatic conditions are not in its favour. The Norwegian Polar Institute and the Norwegian Ministry of Justice in Oslo weren't in favour either and both warned the team that the whole idea was ridiculous. In addition, the team were advised that owing to the unusual mildness of the winter of 1981-82 general ice conditions were poor.

Nonetheless, the four would-be explorers set out for Longyearbyen on Spitsbergen, where they arrived on 26th February 1982 by SAS jet and were welcomed with a good-luck bouquet of flowers from the Spanish Embassy in Oslo. This bouquet was probably the nicest thing that happened to them during their stay. A few days later, a freight aircraft flew in the expedition equipment, many items of which had been damaged in the air because of faulty packing. In temperatures of about -30C, the

173

team set up camp – a tent fixed to an inflatable raft, which they planned to use on the trip.

After the long build-up, the uncomfortable climb-down.

The Governor of Svalbard announced that the equipment was quite unsuitable for a polar expedition. The motorcycles were demonstrably incapable of negotiating ice. On a test run near Longyearbyen airport, one motorcycle pulling a sledge with only 150 kg of equipment had difficulty in maintaining any movement at all, and in the end the sledge overturned. The sledges, which were planned to carry 500 kg apiece, including about 350 litres of petrol, proved weak and badly constructed.

Public opinion began to rumble. Why take so much trouble over a suicide attempt, the locals could be heard thinking, especially when a million kroner could come in so handy for other purposes? The Spaniards at last tumbled to the rumble. Demoralisation was added to disorganisation and within two weeks the expedition plan had been smothered, pummelled and swept off course as though hit by a particularly sentient glacier.

The team never left town with all their kit and not a single motorcycle-sledge combination got away from the airport. The Spaniards tried to sell the motorcycles, not before collecting a reprimand from the Governor for riding the machines in Longyearbyen on 'non-expedition duties'. Anyway, there was no sale: motor-cycles of 100 c.c. are the largest permitted in the settlement. The sledges were left behind, one of them now standing outside the town museum, where it occupies a place of honour.

Which is more than one can say for its owners who, on 12th March, gave up and went home. Great place for motorcycling, Spain.

Land of Ice ... and Fire

Dave and Adam were members of an expedition to Mývatn, Iceland, but on a side trip of their own. They were camped near the ten-metre chasm of Stóragjá.

One morning Dave sat in the doorway of the tent stirring porridge. From his perch he could see steam from the naturally-heated groundwater floating up from the great fissure. Adam struggled from his sleeping bag and, wrapping a towel round his waist in a flourish of true English modesty, went off for an early morning dip in the warm water.

Mývatn is noted for its birdlife and it was no surprise to Dave to see a gyr falcon winging its way across the lake. Interest aroused, he switched off the Primus, placed it just outside the tent and set off with his binoculars.

Three minutes later the falcon had gone. So had the tent. When Dave turned around, a spiral of smoke was all that remained. In three minutes flat he had lost the tent, sleeping bags, clothes – the lot. A gust of wind must have blown the tent flap across the top of the still-hot Primus and instantly ignited.

Dave was thunderstruck. Then a ray of cheer broke through his gloom. Any moment now, he realised, the naked swimmer, oblivious to the disaster, would emerge from the chasm, all set to retrieve his clothes and begin the day's work ...

HOW NOT TO SET A GLIDING RECORD (AND STILL ENJOY CHRISTMAS)

The history of gliding is dotted with comical calamities, auspicious accidents and stark surprises. When the sport was in its infancy (just as, for example, microlight flying is today), amateurism and amusement were top. Failure – even to get a machine off the ground – was common, but then the unpredictability of the thing was a large part of its fun.

Lionel Alexander, a veteran pilot, recalls that happy era when glider pilots took (and liked) pretty much whatever came their way:

"The Cambridge University Gliding Club has always prided itself on its experimental activities. In 1952, the commonest accepted way of keeping a glider in the air was to make use of hill lift – air blowing over a hill and deflected upwards. With luck, you could soar to twice the height of the hill. But rumours were current about strange phenomena in the lee of mountain ranges. When conditions were right, the lucky pilot experienced a lift of eerie smoothness extending to ten or even twenty times the height of the mountains. Standing waves, they came to be called. There were thought to be waves off Snowdonia. By a happy coincidence, the Clwydian range that divides north Wales from England is the right distance to leeward of Snowdonia in a west wind. By an even happier coincidence, a fellow maniac called Bill Crease had recently forsworn engineering in favour of a hotel halfway up a Clwyd near Ruthin. It was called the Clwyd Gate. You could, without excessive hazard, catapult a glider out of the hotel chicken run into the hill lift and thence (we hoped) into the wave lift. Bill was exceedingly hospitable, and had no objection to receiving glider pilots at 3 am.

The winter was reputed to be a good time for waves, so we decided on a Christmas expedition. Because we were anxious to impart our experience to undergraduates, we elected to take the Kranich. This was an enormous high-performance two-seater of German wartime design but built in Czechoslovakia. One of our more enterprising members had liberated it. It was very beautiful and delightful to fly, but it had two disadvantages. First, it was a nightmare to put together. Second, its trailer was massive, mainly because it had been built from cheap secondhand materials. These included an old lorry axle. In all respects, strength had won hands down over lightness.

The cars of those days were hopelessly inadequate to tow this mastodon – anyway, none of us had a serviceable car. So we decided on the Beaver. The Standard Beaverette was a sample of higher technology with which Dad's Army had been supplied if it was lucky. Take a 1939 Standard 12 chassis. Encase it in armour plate. Top it off with a machine gun, and you were all set to repel the invading Panzers. We could get Beavers for a few pounds from our breaker friend. By cutting off most of the armour plate, you were left with an open, slow, unwieldy but cheap vehicle. It was 5.30 am and freezing hard when David and I arrived at Cambridge airport to collect the Beaver and trailer. The Beaver's battery was, as usual, flat. Never mind, we had a small Chevrolet chassis. That, too, had a flat battery, but it had a serviceable starting handle. Unfortunately, the nearly solid oil in the sump effectively prevented hand starting. Back to Cambridge, wake up a posse of fellow-members, return to site, push the Chev. for 50 metres or so. It fired. All that remained was to find some rope, attach the Chev. to the Beaver, tow the Beaver until it fired, put the Chev. to bed, service the Beaver, attach the Kranich trailer and set off.

Our morale at this stage was high, because the physical activity had warmed us. Not for long. Even at 50 kmph, which was all the Beaver would do towing a trailer, the damp chill of a Cambridge winter soon ate through our clothing, flying helmets and goggles notwithstanding, for there was not even a windscreen to protect us. The prospect of a ten-hour journey with snow forecast in Wales did not improve matters. Consequently when, an hour and a half from Cambridge and just outside Thrapston, the Beaver came terminally to a stop with a connecting rod through the crank-case, we had no difficulty in concluding that we had a problem. At this point, however, Father Christmas arrived in the form of Glyn, a fellow club-member. He was driving towards Cambridge on his lawful occasions and stopped when he recognised the Beaver and trailer. This he subsequently regretted. From our point of view however his arrival was a godsend. His vehicle was a Jeep, and, what is more, it had been fitted with an estate car body. Best of all, Jeeps have four-wheel-drive. An appeal to Glyn's club spirit resulted in the original expedition members setting off in triumph towards Wales with Jeep and trailer, while Glyn was left to make his way to Cambridge as best he could, there to organise the profitable disposal of what was left of the Beaver, or alternatively to acquire and fit a replacement engine.

On the next eight hours or so, there is little to report. Reasonably warm and comfortable, David and I plodded on at a dignified 50 kmph. As we entered Wales, snow began to fall promptly on cue, but, armed with the vehicle that won the war, we felt equal to all possible road conditions. Some 30 km from Bill's hotel is the Horseshoe Pass. This pretty road makes exciting driving at the best of times, but with thirty cm of fresh snow on the road, it was too much for us. The Jeep may be a 'go anywhere' vehicle, but there are limits. These we only discovered well into the pass, and on a sharp climbing bend. The wheels slipped, the combination stopped, and then, slowly but inexorably, slid backwards until the trailer jack-knifed, thus putting paid to any further progress and also blocking the pass. It was by this time about midnight, and a noble blizzard was blowing out of the northeast. We uncoupled the trailer and immobilised it, though in the circumstances this was a work of supererogation. The Jeep, unencumbered by the hopeless handicap it had borne up till then, sailed up the pass with little difficulty. At what was for us and for Bill the perfectly reasonable hour of 1.30 am we drove into the hotel car park and accepted whisky, supper and coffee.

After supper, there was chat and chaff. At about 3 am, it occurred to us that something ought to be done about the trailer. The suggestion that something might be attempted with Bill's Beaver and the Jeep in tandem was rejected as impractical, so we telephoned the police. Not unreasonably, the reaction of a sleepy duty officer to the news that the only local road into Wales was likely to be impassable for some time was less than ecstatic. Eventually he pulled himself together and, in his musical north Welsh lilt, he enquired where we were. To the direct question, there was no alternative to the truth. "We are with Mr Crease at the Clwyd Gate", I said, with forebodings of a night in the nick for all three of us. "Ah, Mr Crease – then that will be quite alright" came the reply. And so it was. Whether the officer in question had ceased to marvel at Bill's doings, or had listened to the weather forecast, I shall never know.

A week later, the end of our holiday coincided with a thaw. The police helped us dig out the trailer, saw us safely bound for Cambridge, and, with some ceremony, reopened the pass. It didn't matter. During the entire week, northerlies with snow showers continued. Flying was out of the question. The undergraduates never arrived, but we had a lovely white Christmas.

It was not until two years later that, on a glorious early spring day, and in a single-seater, I lifted off out of the chicken run. I dodged the trees, fought my way up the mountain in rough, broken lift and, half an hour later, suddenly felt everything go smooth. I watched, fascinated, holding my breath and hardly daring to move the controls, while the altimeter steadily wound round to 2,750 metres. It was my first wave."

OUTWARD BOUND

At 18, Richard J. Scheuer, of Andover, New Jersey, was bored. Unlike some others of his generation, he did not channel his surplus energy into the dismantling of public property or the disfiguring of private individuals. In his case, the solution took the form of trying to hike from Rankin Inlet, on the western shore of Hudson Bay, in Canada's Northwest Territories, to Nome, Alaska, a distance, as the Arctic Skua might fly, of some 3,500 km.

He dropped out of college, worked, saved and in June 1978, then aged nineteen, set off.

When he arrived in Rankin, a quick inventory of his equipment revealed that one of his tent poles had broken in half. He mended it with duct tape but it would not give the support needed to keep the canvas taut, with the result that the rainfly caved up against the tent and he was showered with gushing water every morning from the build-up of condensation on the tent roof.

The spring thaw normally occurs in the Arctic around mid-May. In 1978 it chose to occur in mid-June and the rivers were brimming over with icy water. The smaller streams could be crossed easily enough barefoot but the Meladine River was a different kettle of fish. With marvellous anticipation, Scheuer had brought a raft with him. Unfortunately, his foresight hadn't extended to testing it in advance. Unable to support the weight of passenger and backpack, the raft sank about ten metres from the shore. Scheuer spent the next two days trying to find a section of the river that could be waded, but the further upstream he went the wider the river became. A lightning flash of insight told him that even if he crossed the Meladine there were innumerable other rivers that would have to be negotiated between here and Nome. It was this realisation that made him abort the trip.

In March 1980 he flew back to Rankin for another try. Airline handling systems being the same in the frozen north as elsewhere in the world, his luggage arrived instead in Thompson, and a three-day delay ensued before Scheuer and his backpack were reunited. His planned route was to take him as far as Baker Lake on hard windpacked snow which he hoped would be 'just like walking on a sidewalk'. It wasn't altogether like that. At first, he encountered deep, soft snow. Then there was a section of pressure ice full of hidden cracks and crevasses. He stepped into one of these but his backpack, wedging against the ice, stopped him from falling right through. On his third day out he found himself on new ice, which bent awesomely under every step. When the 'give' became giving way, Scheuer slid slowly but helplessly into the water. Clutching at a block of ice, he hauled himself out – and plodded on.

A day or two later he met a group of Eskimos in a tracked vehicle who informed him that the ice further north was all broken up and advised him to follow their tracks to Chesterfield. Scheuer left the pack ice and headed for land, where he found the snow at best ankle-deep and at worst knee-deep. Frostbite began to nibble at his face and feet and he had a nasty cut, sustained while cleaning ice out of his tent poles. When next a couple of Eskimos came by, in a snowmobile, it was time to admit defeat and catch a lift. Wearing borrowed windproof trousers, *kamiks* (Eskimo shoes), a parka and rabbit skin mittens, he travelled on their supply sled which lurched wildly as it jumped snow drifts and often almost tipped him out.

A three-day stay with an Eskimo family in Chesterfield Inlet, while he waited for the flight that would bring this second attempt to a close, was the unexpected highlight of the whole episode.

The great adventure had fizzled out into two minor failures. All was not lost, though. Richard Scheuer had given boredom a swift kick in the seat, and when last heard of it was alive and well and living in Nome, Alaska.

BEATEN BY THE DRUMS

A 200-litre oil drum is about a metre long and 60cms in diameter. Weld three of these together, end to end, and you have a tube. Cut a hole about 45cms square in the top of the centre drum, and you have a place to sit in the tube – always providing you get in knees first and squat in the 'cockpit' first before stretching your legs out in front of you.

The next stage, if you're Estonian-born Peter Pedaja, alias Stanley Lexton, is to put to sea in this object. Pedaja insisted that the D.S. (= drift ship) *Wakefield* – so called because the drums once contained oil made by the firm of that name – was a craft and not a raft, since one rode *in* and not *on* it.

As first constructed, the *Wakefield* had no motor, no sail, not even a keel for stability. So when Pedaja set out in it on the tides from Darwin in 1957, bound for Timor, it wasn't long before he capsized. He quickly discovered that in this situation the mariner himself had to serve as a keel. Hanging upside down in the water with 'a fish's eye view of the fish', he found the cockpit just as difficult to get out of as it was to get into. The ninety seconds he spent extricating himself, like some salt water-saturated Houdini, convinced him of the need to modify his vessel.

Pedaja spent a few more coins on a couple of extra oil

drums and lashed them on to the existing creation – one on either side of the rear drum. This gave the now T-shaped craft a two-metre width at the stern. It also cramped his paddling style and interfered with his 'purchase' on the water. His seafaring equipment consisted of a compass which, proving faulty, was made to walk the plank, and a billycan, not for making tea but for bailing.

Pedaja then packed his legs, along with seven tins of meat, seven of fruit and 22 litres of water, back into the 'control' drum and cast his hopes to the winds – and tides. "Just before dawn," he recalled, "the tide reached full flood, then lifted me and carried me out as it ebbed. I had no trouble this time in staying upright. I began paddling and drifting out to sea. At daylight I still wasn't past Darwin Heads, but about two hours later I saw East Point drifting behind and I knew then that I was on the way to Timor ... or wherever the currents were going to take me". The *Wakefield* proved buoyant and seaworthy, behaving so well that "I didn't get one drop of water in the cockpit the whole time I was at sea.'

After a night alone, our adventurer, for reasons best known to himself, had a change of mind. And, with it, a change of direction. He turned round and headed back towards Darwin. "I realised that I wasn't quite ready for this thing", he said. It also struck him that a sail would be useful, to say the least, for crossing an ocean. Also, rather late in the day (though actually very early in the morning), he remembered that he owed money and wanted to clear his debts before he left Australia.

Getting back there wasn't easy, with the tides and currents adopting a contrary point of view. *Wakefield* was being drawn further out to sea, despite its navigator's efforts at paddling. The second night out passed in fitful sleep, Pedaja having to remind himself constantly not to let an arm trail in the water as a temptation to cruising sharks. He remained out of sight of land, though by his estimate only about 30km offshore.

Mistaken by a passing vessel for a buoy – until the buoy waved its arms – the craft was picked up and towed back to Darwin. Dejected, Pedaja travelled back on board the ship.

This should have been the end of the story, but wasn't, thanks to Pedajan persistence. He continued to dream about putting to sea in a longer, better-equipped drift ship with a sail and a hatch over the cockpit. This way, he reasoned, the craft would be like a sealed tin. It would be unsinkable! He would become the first man to travel around the world in a craft made of oil drums!

At that point, fate and the king tides intervened. Pedaja had taken a job on the vessel that had picked him up and was saving up for improvements to his own craft. Then, one August night, it simply vanished. Riding the swirling eight-metre tides, it made an unscheduled, unmanned departure from Darwin for points unknown, and was never seen again.

Come Wind or Fairweather
In June 1952 a Scottish-born artist named Ian Fairweather crossed the Timor Sea from Darwin on a two-metre raft built of driftwood and aircraft belly tanks. To make the first such passage was peculiar enough. Even odder was Peter Pedaja's faith in the value of attempting a *second* voyage of that sort.

CAVING, KAMIKAZE STYLE

Caving is a bit like mountaineering upside down. The two sports use very similar techniques, but in caving the ultimate difficulty lies not in reaching the furthermost point from ground level, but in getting back again. Flash floods, underground streams, protruding ledges, faulty breathing apparatus and mere gravity can all hamper the caver's progress up towards the surface.

There is another problem in caving that sets it apart from mountaineering. A mountain can be surveyed, measured and photographed from various angles; routes can be plotted up it, obstacles foreseen and avoided, the environment observed and its prevailing weather charted – all before, sometimes years before, the mountain explorer actually sets foot upon it. Not so in caving: here the processes of discovery and of physical exploration occur simultaneously. Cavers never know what they are going to find, nor whether they can bring both themselves and news of their discoveries back to ground level.

So cavers should be not only skilled and well equipped but also circumspect and flexible to a fault.

Enter the G Parachute Light Battery (Mercer's Troops) Royal Horse Artillery. It is June 1968 and the scene is the extreme northwest of Greece, where a deep shaft, known locally as Provatina, has been partially explored but not 'bottomed' by various parties since its discovery by a Cambridge University reconnaissance team in 1962. The Army unit has equipment and manpower, optimism and crude confidence in boundless supply. Among other things, it has brought along a heavy petrol-driven winch which has taken nine days to 'drive' to the site under its own power. Attached to the winch is a helicopter air/sea rescue 'bosun's chair' and in it, in this case, is the engineer who designed and constructed it. Whether he has volunteered for this position or not is unknown.

Now imagine, if you can, the internal configuration of a cave that nobody has ever fully seen, surveyed or explored.

Difficult, isn't it? What shape could the entrance shaft

be? – freefall?, angled?, corkscrew? Are there any ledges on which a cable might catch or a chair get wedged or tip over? Is the shaft wide enough to take a chair with a person in it, comfortably, at any speed? How far down might the bottom of the shaft be? What is to be found at the bottom of the cave? – a deep pool, perhaps, into which the unfortunate 'explorer' in the chair might be lowered? And are there any passages leading off from the bottom of the entrance shaft which might be worthy of further exploration and could indeed give access to still deeper sections of the cave?

Without fully knowing answers to any of these questions and with a breezy 'anyone for disaster?' approach, the Army unit went ahead and lowered their man down the shaft. They took no safety precautions; there was no possibility of communication between the man in the chair and the team on the ground; and they were to rely entirely on relaxation of tension on the cable as a sign that the chair had reached the floor.

Well, with an oversized and wholly undeserved portion of luck, they did it. The 'victim' reached the bottom of the shaft where he was allowed ten minutes, precisely timed, to look around before being hauled up again. The entrance shaft turned out to be a sheer drop of 396 m, then the deepest known single pitch in the world, and the bottom to be only 8.5m further down, at 404 m.

The team chalked it up as a success – and maybe in one way it was. The Royal Horse Artillery rode roughshod over the ethics and standards of caving, had faint regard for their own safety and in exploration terms produced a lightly moistened squib. But perhaps providence has a sneaking admiration for enthusiasm. They got away with it – and that alone was no small matter.

DEFLATED HOPES

It took Paul Parsons four years to arrive at the beginning of his adventure and only 36 hours to arrive at its end.

Parsons, a 29-year-old qualified diver and underwater photographer from Feltham, Middlesex, sold his house and car to raise £4,500 to finance his planned solo crossing of the Atlantic in an inflatable rubber boat. He obtained part-sponsorship from a clothing manufacturer and six months' leave of absence from his employers, Air Canada. He carried out trials in the Irish Sea with his 5.3-metre-long boat, an extensively adapted version of the inflatable craft used in shooting rapids in the Grand Canyon. It was fitted with lee boards on either side, a rudder, a sail and self-steering gear. As well as a puncture repair kit, Parsons was carrying a radio and emergency beacons. He experimented with a bag which would be attached to the top of the boat's mast and would automatically inflate to prevent the craft from being wholly overturned.

Obviously, he said, this was "not a joke ... not something I am doing for a gimmick. I want to sail the Atlantic in a rubber boat because it has not been done before. An Irishman tried it in 1977 but his boat flipped while he was asleep about 480 km from shore".

The voyage was to take 60 days and cover 4,480 km.

Alas, the best laid schemes of masts and men oft go astray. Parsons' ambition was wrecked by a whale smashing the floorboards of the dinghy just 36 hours after he left Halifax, Nova Scotia, in June 1979. The rudder came adrift and was lost and the boat began to let in water. Parsons sent out a distress signal and was picked up by a fishing boat.

The bubble burst, in more ways than one.

FULL FRONTAL DEFENCE

In the 1950s, the two-seater distance record in a glider was only about seventy km. The single-seater record stood at around 560 km. All it needed was for some men of resolve to go and break the records.

Cambridge University was full of men of resolve, not to mention intellectual brilliance, practical sang-froid and imperturbable self-confidence. The idea of taking on the two-seater record had been knocking around the Committee of the Gliding Club ever since the Kranich had arrived, but it was not until two young men, both named David, joined forces that an attempt came to be made.

The Kranich was supposed to have been built in Germany and repatriated by enthusiastic glider pilots serving in the forces of occupation. Now, however, it was at Cambridge on indefinite loan. It was a magnificent machine. Its wings spread eighteen metres in a graceful gull form. The two flyers sat one in front of the wing spar, the other just behind. It had a deep fuselage on a single landing skid, and it was so heavy that two small droppable wheels were fitted to the skid so that the sailplane could be launched more easily.

It was agreed that David One, a Flight Lieutenant in the RAF, flying instructor and postgraduate student, would be pilot in charge; David Two, an undergraduate and Gliding Club senior instructor, his navigator. They took off one bright sunny morning with their course marked out towards the southeast for a flight of 175 km, quite far enough to beat the record by a respectable margin, but not so far that they couldn't come and break it again later that summer, perhaps in the Nationals.

Not so easy as it seemed. David One did the launch and found a thermal, but he wasn't satisfied, so they went to another. That wasn't too good either, but by the time they got back to where the first one had been it had gone; anyway, David Two said later, from the point of view of safety they were too low to use it. Twenty minutes after the launch they were down in a field on the other side of the airfield boundary, quite near a housing estate.

David One took charge immediately they stopped rolling across the light loam. "David," he instructed his friend, "I am the pilot and will guard the aircraft. You are navigator and will go for the trailer".

David Two obediently trotted off across the field, over the hedge and back to the hangar to join the knot of people there who had watched them land.

It took them all of twenty minutes to get the trailer hitched to the truck and into the field to collect the now dormant Kranich. Angela was with them. She was a nice bright girl who flew quite well and came down on Saturdays. She went around the sailplane on the southern side a little ahead of the group. She gave a little scream and stopped in her tracks.

David One, in a voice that displayed every ounce of the intellectual and cultural superiority he had at his disposal, explained loftily: "I thought it would keep the spectators away". The others, rounding the bend, soon saw what 'it' was: David had taken off all his clothing and stood there, unabashed, without a stitch.

STATELY PLEASURE-DOME

A balloon is a registered aircraft and as such its pilot is subject to aviation law in the same way as the captain of an international jet airliner. But one thing this childishly simple law does not define is the term 'air'. The air is above us, of course. No problem, on the face of it. But there is air underground too, isn't there? What about flying underground? Would legislators sink so low?

Certainly, Squadron Leader Roly R. Parsons and his colleagues from the Royal New Zealand Air Force would.

In New Zealand there sits a relatively little known but nevertheless spectacular cavern, called the Hollow Hill Cave. Long, high and tunnel-shaped, the cave could comfortably accommodate an oceangoing liner. It has mud lower walls, a stream running through it, all the usual stalactites and stalagmites and a colony of glow-worms, enjoying life and minding their own business. Parsons and pals, ballooning fanatics to a man, conceived the idea of flying their balloon, *West Wind*, inside the cavern.

The local Ranger was enthusiastic about the scheme and the public imagination was caught too, though the team, jealous of their secret, had done their best to avoid attracting attention. They set about studying the cave for its potential. To overcome the obstacle of the running stream, they proposed to build a large platform of tubular scaffolding over which tarpaulins would be stretched to make a base from which to launch the balloon.

The appeal of the venture became more and more magnetic. Not only would the balloon be able to float around at the push of a finger, since there are no wind currents in a cave, but there was the added challenge of flying at night, which is normally illegal in that other air above the ground. Then too the plan was full of aesthetic and photographic promise: the balloon would be illuminated like a great Chinese lantern, the reds and yellows of its burner lighting up the fabric and darting flickers and reflections about the bizarre background of the cavern. The cave formations would take on new and fascinating shapes and shades; and the glow-worms would stir themselves from their everyday duties and look on ...

Just when Roly Parsons was in the final phase of converting the dream to reality – getting the scaffolding together, setting up the photo-floods and the tarpaulins and collecting the gear – an urgent letter was delivered to him at his Wellington office. It came from the Minister of Lands himself, Mr. Kenn Young. The environmental action lobby – a faceless and nameless group who usually do the necessary and occasionally even a little more – had bent his ear. The Minister of the crown informed Sqn. Ldr. Parsons, in his best official manner, that the axe of State had fallen upon his project. The powers-that-be had issued a let-them-be decree on behalf of the poor put-upon glow-worms: they were to be left in peace. And so the Hollow Hill Cave project never got off, or under, the ground.

This is very often what happens when one takes an idea through all the proper channels. Many adventurers have drawn their own conclusions about the wisdom of seeking advance permission. Doubtless Parsons and his friends are aware of this: who knows what other dark plans they might be hatching?

A PETRE-FLYING EXPERIENCE

Aircraft have always been valuable items, but perhaps never more so than in the early days of aviation, when a single machine had to do triple service as a prototype, test plane and production model. Losing one of these aircraft was like breaking the mould: there was no other like it to take its place.

One such machine was the Handley Page monoplane nicknamed 'the Yellow Peril'. Prior to the First World War, there were no test pilots as such and many aviators were as unpractised as the machines were untried. Yet careless exhibitionism was the order of the day. To Edward Petre, who exemplified this spirit, the irreplaceable 'Yellow Peril' was an irresistible temptation.

One day (since he happened to have the opportunity),

he got up, without a word, sauntered over to the plane and climbed in. He tried the controls, worked the empennage (tail section) and manoeuvred the rudder. Then he opened the engine up full. When the aircraft nearly went over the chocks, his colleagues suddenly caught on to his intentions.

"What are you up to, Edward?" they demanded to know. "What the devil are you up to there? Come out! Come out!"

But Edward took no notice. He simply revved up, went over the chocks, taxied for about two hundred metres and took off. In the air he flew the machine like an experienced pilot. He turned it round, climbed and headed off. The next thing his pals knew was that he'd landed at Brooklands aerodrome, where he was questioned by an official, severely reprimanded and charged with flying an aircraft without a licence.

It was true he had no licence. It was also true that this was the first time he had ever been in the air.

TIGER IN THE CORN

The Dawn to Dusk Rally is organised in Britain annually by the Tiger Club, a trophy being awarded, usually by the Chief Judge, HRH Prince Philip, to the team who have made the best possible use of a light plane for one whole day, dawn to dusk, during the month of June.

In 1980, Charles Shea-Simonds won the Duke of Edinburgh Trophy with a project that traced the history of aviation in Yorkshire. In 1981, with his co-pilot Julie Hanks, he won again, flying for fifteen hours between 4.30 a m and 9 p m, in an attempt to fly to every county in the country, with landings on farmers' airstrips only. They achieved most of what they had intended, with forty-three landings in forty-three different counties.

Immediately, Charlie and Julie, with only a year to go

until the 1982 event, began intensive planning for their next project, in the hope of scoring the first ever hat-trick in the history of the Rally. Did they think they'd win again? asked Prince Philip, voicing everybody's question. No, replied Charlie, he didn't think His Highness would let them!

As it turned out, fate and the British weather took precedence over the royal assent.

The project for 1982 centred around an aeroplane rather than an idea: the DH82A Tiger Moth, the Tiger Club's own plane. Fifty years old in 1982, GA–CDC – known to its friends as 'CDC' – was the oldest Tiger Moth on the British Register. The aims were threefold, but seemed to grow more elaborate in detail as the preparations proceeded: to visit places with de Havilland and Tiger Moth connections; to fly into three airfields belonging respectively to the Army, the Navy and the Air Force, in tribute to the services which used the Tiger Moth as a basic trainer in wartime; and to create a nostalgic feeling for aviation as it was fifty years ago, with a visit to each of six well known stately homes. To this end, Shea-Simonds was to wear white flannels, a white jumper, a long leather coat, a leather helmet, and carry a boater in the luggage compartment for donning at suitable moments throughout the day.

The weather in June 1982 was extraordinary. Anti-cyclones were the norm, with thick early morning fog and mist. For the day of the Rally, the 8th, the forecast was much the same, although a check at 3.30 am revealed that the fog, expected especially in the Thames Valley, might be somewhat less troublesome than on previous days, and promised that improved conditions would be found the further west one went.

Preparations had reached a climax during the two days prior to the Rally and the aircraft had been brought for the start to Hatfield, Herts., its place of construction fifty years earlier. Leo Dickinson and crew were there ready to film this project for Independent Television. On the interplane struts a camera was rigged up which could be operated from the cockpit, and the two pilots flew some practice runs to test both CDC and camera.

The projected route took them southwest to Seven Barrows, a downland area just south of Newbury, Berks., where Geoffrey de Havilland had made his first flight in 1910. There they would make a quick circuit of the field, salute de Havilland's memorial at its edge, and fly on to Thruxton, where they would rendezvous with Charles' father. Shea-Simonds Senior would be in a Jackaroo, a descendant of the Tiger Moth, which he had been first to fly in the mid-1950s.

CDC started at the second swing of the propeller, as usual, and they were off, in the half-light, flying west. There were plenty of grey clouds about but a bit of a silver lining too. How many people have the opportunity to prove the Met. Office diametrically, dramatically and disastrously wrong? Visibility, which at the outset was about 6–8 km, declined steadily as they flew over High Wycombe and Booker Airfield, along the Thames Valley and towards Newbury. The cloud thickened above, the fog below. They had now lost contact with the ground. Observation and common sense told them to call off the flight; the weather forecast rang in their ears, telling them to press on.

By the time they were six km past Newbury, however, conditions had deteriorated to breaking point. Going back had little to recommend it and, as they discovered later, the aerodrome at Hatfield had also been closed in by fog. Their only course of action became as clear as the weather was not. Unless they were going to be 'caught out in a big way' and try to put down in solid fog, they had to land now.

Shea-Simonds cast around for a landing site. Through a break in the mist he spotted an open area of farmland, about 300 metres long, on which grew what he took to be grass. He headed for it, made an approach and came in. What looked like grass turned out to be standing corn nearly a metre tall. Too late! The corn plucked at the wheels and, as CDC decelerated, turned her, gently as a caress, onto her back. The propeller shattered as it came into contact with the ground and the engine stopped. In the cockpit, kept off the ground by the biplane's upper wing, hung Charlie and Julie in their harnesses, upside down.

Curiously enough, neither was injured. On later inspection, CDC's fin and rudder were found to be substantially damaged, her propeller gone and her near fuselage slightly bent, but overall her condition was not as bad as they had feared.

Which did not alter the fact that Shea-Simonds and his partner were out of the Rally, their participation having lasted from dawn to . . . just after dawn.

The rest of the day and the better part of the next were spent in righting the plane, taking off her wings, towing the fuselage behind a Cortina and carrying the wings on a roof-rack to a nearby farm, loading her onto a trailer and eventually taking her back to Redhill, in Surrey, her home base.

Meanwhile, Leo Dickinson and his team, the police and a local newshound all appeared on the scene, where their main accomplishment was to rub salt into the wound. The police were somewhat ill at ease, since no-one had been hurt, no other party's property had been damaged and the Civil Aviation Authority assured them that they wished to take no action. They came, shifted uncomfortably from one foot to the other, and went again. The reporter arrived after the wings had been unscrewed, assumed they had come off in the crash and filed a rather sensational story with the *Newbury Times*.

Dickinson's first thought was to ask whether Charlie and Julie had shot film of the 'landing'. No, they said, they'd had one or two other things to think about at the time. Pity, mused Dickinson; if they'd got good footage, the television company would probably have paid them enough to buy another plane. Determined to salvage something from the fiasco, Dickinson was to be seen by laughter-convulsed onlookers later that day trying to simulate CDC's brush with the corn by somersaulting across the field, a camera held high above his head.

A Bath in the Wash

What are an unemployed man, a barman and an engineer doing in a bath together?

You guessed it: trying to raise money for medical research.

The three set out from the River Nene to paddle around the east coast of England in the tub, 240 km to Great Yarmouth, Norfolk, in September 1982. When they failed to arrive at Hunstanton, an air-sea rescue operation was launched and they were picked up by the Hunstanton lifeboat as they drifted nine km out into The Wash.

The cost of the rescue amounted to several thousand pounds. Sea rescue experts were not amused, describing the charitable effort variously as 'foolhardy', 'creating trouble for other people' and just plain 'idiotic'.

DO-IT-YOURSELF CRAZY ADVENTURE STORY
(A Game of Consequences)

.... set out on .... to
(name(s))   (date)

glide
drive
ride
sail
climb
parachute
hang-glide
fly
walk
run
ski
pothole
dive
track down
swim
motorcycle
bungy-jump
sledge
shoot
windsurf
hunt
paddle
jump
sit on
stand on

a(n)

raft	from	a building
elephant	to	rapids
wheelbarrow	on	China
high-wire	in	a tree
branch	out of	the M1

monster	down	the Amazon
kayak	up	the sea
toboggan	along	the North Pole
camel	through	the South Pole
Snocat	across	the Atlantic
boat	around	the Pacific
board	under	Australia
car	over	Mt. Everest
motorcycle	in the middle of	Britain
balloon		the USA
cave		the Sahara
cliff		the English
bi-plane		Channel
jet		the world
dog		space
bath		
barrel		
chair		
treasure		
buoy		
shark		

with

snowshoes
bananas
five companions
a fine cheek
a rubber chicken
a helmet-mounted camera
the sponsors' blessing
a flag
a gondola
the Christmas spirit
a team of huskies
ten years' preparation
a shotgun
a bottle of champagne
flippers

packing boxes
a balancing pole
head in the air
£1.49 in loose change
a shotgun
an eye on the record books

He
She   was
They   were

snowed in
chased by a gunman
naked
over retiring age
wrecked
disowned by his mother
filmed
rescued
bored rigid
blown off course
ecstatic
stranded
capsized
attacked by a bear
foiled
arrested
in the headlines
burnt
sunk
successful
injured
disappointed
fêted
vilified
never the same again
blind drunk at the time

and the consequence was. . . . .
. . . .(entirely up to you)

SOURCES

ALL MANNER OF MEANS

Higher, Faster and Miura — *Observer*, 7.9.1975

Germany's Fruit and Nut Case — Klaus Höppner; Rüdiger Nehberg

Chariots of Snow — Jaume Llansana

Seventeen Months on the Trot — *Observer Magazine*, 12.6.1977

Bought a Crooked Cat, Sailed a Crooked Mile — D.H. Clarke

Wheelered Vehicles — Jack Wheeler: *The Adventurer's Guide*, David McKay Co. Inc., New York; *Time*, 1.10.1979

Bulldog Drummond and the Mystery of the Pyramid — Jeff Long: "In the Constellation of Roosters and Lunatics", *Ascent* magazine, USA

French Duel on the Atlantic — Christian Marty; Gerard d'Aboville; *Surf* magazine, Munich, West Germany; Ari Barshi

Cliffers — Robin Heid; Doug Buchanan; Randy Leavitt

Jaume, Joan, Josep – and Jules — Jaume Llansana

Underwater Risibility — Fred Walton: "Underwater Hang Gliding", *Diver* magazine, July 1982

Ready, Willig and Abe — Thomas C. Young, World Trade Center, New York

Daly of Delight — Maj. Warwick Deacock

"All Goes if Courage Goes" Ted Lewington

Shorter items
Anything You Canoe Do, I Canoe Do Better *Paddlers World* newsletter, 1982
Formidable Feet *Daily Telegraph*, 25 and 26.8.1978
Making Waves *Daily Telegraph*, 11.2.1983
Sailing Through Paris Christian-Yves Nau: *Le Désert en Char à Voile*, éditions PAC, Paris, 1980
Trans-Siberian Russian *The Guinness Book of Records*
Taste for Adventure John Hunt: *The Ascent of Everest*, Hodder & Stoughton, London 1953

TRY ANYTHING ONCE

Wild Thing One Alan Byde
How Brazilian Ballooning Went Like a Bomb Robert J. Rechs
Make Straight in the Desert a Highway Richard Slowe: *Innocents in Africa*, Royal Automobile Club, London, 1978; Lord Hunt
Filming the Unlikely *TV Times*, December 1980; Leo Dickinson; *Filming the Impossible*, Hodder & Stoughton, London, 1982
The Curate's Egg *Time*, 18.11.1974; *To the Point International*, 11.1.1975; *The Times*, 2.4.1975

Wild West Fjord	Knut Hoff

Shorter items

Blue Coats Over the White Cliffs of Dover	Mick Fowler: "Chalking Up", *Mountain* No. 85, May/June 1982; T.I.M. Lewis
Salisbury Plane	Philip Berent
Stunted Stunt	R. Simpson, RAF Museum, Hendon

STRANGER THAN FICTION

Escape into Escapism	Felice Benuzzi: *No Picnic on Mount Kenya: The Story of Three PoWs' Escape to Adventure*, William Kimber, London, 1952
Vehicle Vessels	*Observer*, 22.10.1978; *Daily Telegraph*, 4.7.1981
Failure of Belief	Walt Unsworth: *Everest*, Allen Lane, London, 1981; Charles Warren's diary; *Telegraph Sunday Magazine*, 9.11.1980
The Headman Who Could Panda to American Tastes	Peter Byrne
Abominable Sandman	Major Charles Weston-Baker; Sqn Ldr Roly Parsons
Huge Monster Not Seen in the Himalayas	Ralph Izzard; Peter Byrne
Beyond the Pale	Dr Andrés Solanot

INVENTION AND INTERVENTION

Shorter items

Banana Split	Bill Johnson: "The Day We Went Bananas", Long Range Desert Group Association *Newsletter* No. 28, 1982; Dr. Mark Milburn
Mad Englishman Out in the Midday Sun	Dr. Hal Lister
Self-Supporting Salesman	D.H. Clarke
Take a Partner	*The Canoe-Camper* magazine, January 1950; Oliver Cock
The Call of the Bluff	Ed Moody: "Fabulous Failures", *Treasure Search* magazine, Cal., USA

CHARACTERS

Legends in their Own Lifelines	David Kirke
Japanese Expertise Out in Front	*The Times*, 2.5.1978; *Time*, 1.2.1982
The Happiness-Maker	Philippe Petit and John Reddy: "Two Towers, I Walk", *Reader's Digest*, April 1975; Robin Heid; Thomas C. Young, World Trade Center, New York
Magnum Forbes	*Rocky Mountain News*, 24.10.1982; Robin Heid

How the Faussett Got Turned On	Whit Deschner: *Does the Wet Suit You? The Confessions of a Kayak Bum*, The Eddie Tern Press, Seattle, 1981
Handsome is as Hans Does	*Daily Telegraph* (Australia), 28.11.1972; *Overlander* magazine, Australia, Dec. 1976–Jan. 1977; *Daily Telegraph*, 20.12.1982 and 8.1.1983
Life Jumps Up	Robin Heid
No Bridge Too Far	Per Arne Jeremiassen; Joan Pinkney; Knut Hoff
Fire in the Snow	Guy Waterman; *Alaskan Mountain* magazine, Spring/Summer 1981; *Alaska* magazine, July 1979; *American Alpine Journal*, 1974, 1979 and 1982; Doug Buchanan; T.I.M. Lewis

Shorter items

Heights of Enjoyment	Philip Judson
Pieces of Eight	Robin Heid
The Skiing Tuareg	Simon Glen; Hadji Abderrahmane
The Truth at Last	Maj. Warwick Deacock
Try, Try Again	David Hempleman-Adams; *Daily Telegraph*, Feb.–April 1983
Two-Faced Lady	Gertrude Baskine: *Hitch-Hiking the Alaska Highway*, Macmillan, Toronto, 1944

GOING TO EXTREMES

Going Round the World Makes the World Go Round	David Springbett; *Evening Standard*, 11.1.1980, May 1980, 26.1.1982; Michael Bartlett
Deadly Enemies	John Fairfax: *Britannia: Rowing Alone Across the Atlantic*, William Kimber, London, 1972; John Fairfax and Sylvia Cook: *Oars Across the Pacific. 8,000 Miles by Rowing Boat*, William Kimber, London, 1972
I'm Gringo. Fly Me	Volker Lenzner
Hail the Conquering Anti-Hero	*Time*, 14.10.1974
Born-Again Flyer	Michael Bartlett; *Wings Over Africa* magazine, May 1979; *Business Traveller* magazine, October 1980

Shorter items

Antique Antics	D.H. Clarke
Crossing the Line to Lunacy	confidential
Dead End	Rüdiger Nehberg
Overkill Over the Arctic	Ranulph Fiennes: *Hell on Ice*, Hodder & Stoughton, London, 1979
Swimming Down Britain	BBC *Woman's Hour*, 28.7.1982

CATALOGUES OF DISASTER

Armchair Explorer	*Observer*, 4.7.1982; *Daily Telegraph*, 20.12.1982
Hunter and the *Nimrod* Variation	J. Clarke: *Angmagssalik Round Britain: The Story of Geoffrey Hunter's 2,000 Mile Solo Voyage Around the Coast of Britain in an Eskimo Kayak*, privately published
Spanish Bull	Robin Buzza
How Not to Set a Gliding Record (and Still Enjoy Christmas)	Lionel Alexander
Outward Bound	Richard J. Scheuer; Stuart Shackell
Beaten by the Drums	*People* magazine, Australia, 27.11.1957
Caving, Kamikaze Style	Jim Eyre: *The Cave Explorers*, Stalactite Press, Calgary, Alberta, Canada, 1981; David Judson: *Ghar Parau*, Cassell, London, 1973
Deflated Hopes	*Daily Telegraph*, 9.4.1977 and 18.6.1979
Full Frontal Defence	Chris Riddell
Stately Pleasure-Dome	Sqn Ldr Roly Parsons
A Petre-Flying Experience	R. Simpson, RAF Museum, Hendon
Tiger in the Corn	Charles Shea-Simonds; Leo Dickinson

Shorter items

A Bath in the Wash	*Daily Telegraph*, 15.9.1982
A Czech on Progress	David Pindar; *The Citizen*, Prince George, BC, Canada, 19.7.1978
Come Wind or Fairweather	*People* magazine, Australia, 27.11.1957
Land of Ice . . . and Fire	Tony Escritt
Man and Fireman	Christopher Portway

ACKNOWLEDGEMENTS

It is my pleasure to thank for their help with this book:

all those who entered into the ridiculous spirit of the thing and volunteered information and contacts, whether the items they suggested found their way into the book or not; in particular, for multifarious researches, Robin Heid of Denver, Col., whose broken leg, sustained while parachuting from the 46th floor of a building in that city, is now on the mend;
those who lent illustrations;
my publishers, for their goodwill and enterprise; especially David Harsent, for keeping a watchful eye on the book's progress and for his sensitive and scrupulous editing;
my family, for their forbearance;
humankind in general, for its propensity for acts of lunacy.